INTRODUCING
ISSUES WITH
OPPOSING
VIEWPOINTS®

Oil

Lauri S. Friedman and Jennifer L. Skancke, *Book Editors*

GREENHAVEN PRESS
A part of Gale, Cengage Learning

GALE
CENGAGE Learning™

Detroit • New York • San Francisco • New Haven, Conn • Waterville, Maine • London

Christine Nasso, *Publisher*
Elizabeth Des Chenes, *Managing Editor*

For more information, contact:
Greenhaven Press
27500 Drake Rd.
Farmington Hills, MI 48331-3535
Or you can visit our Internet site at gale.cengage.com

For product information and technology assistance, contact us at

Gale Customer Support, 1-800-877-4253
For permission to use material from this text or product, submit all requests online at www.cengage.com/permissions

Further permissions questions can be emailed to permissionrequest@cengage.com

Articles in Greenhaven Press anthologies are often edited for length to meet page requirements. In addition, original titles of these works are changed to clearly present the main thesis and to explicitly indicate the author's opinion. Every effort is made to ensure that Greenhaven Press accurately reflects the original intent of the authors. Every effort has been made to trace the owners of copyrighted material.

Cover image © 2008/Jupiterimages

LIBRARY OF CONGRESS CATALOGING-IN-PUBLICATION DATA

Friedman, Lauri S.
  Oil / Lauri S. Friedman and Jennifer L. Skancke, book editors.
    p. cm. — (Introducing issues with opposing viewpoints)
  Includes bibliographical references and index.
  ISBN-13: 978-0-7377-4171-1 (hardcover) 1. Petroleum. 2. Petroleum reserves. 3. Fuel switching. I. Skancke, Jennifer. II. Title.
  TN870.F77776 2008
  553.2'82—dc22
                                                                      2008011155

Printed in the United States of America
1 2 3 4 5 6 7 12 11 10 09 08

Contents

Chapter 3: Should Oil Be Replaced with Other Energy Sources?

Foreword

Indulging in a wide spectrum of ideas, beliefs, and perspectives is a critical cornerstone of democracy. After all, it is often debates over differences of opinion, such as whether to legalize abortion, how to treat prisoners, or when to enact the death penalty, that shape our society and drive it forward. Such diversity of thought is frequently regarded as the hallmark of a healthy and civilized culture. As the Reverend Clifford Schutjer of the First Congregational Church in Mansfield, Ohio, declared in a 2001 sermon, "Surrounding oneself with only like-minded people, restricting what we listen to or read only to what we find agreeable is irresponsible. Refusing to entertain doubts once we make up our minds is a subtle but deadly form of arrogance." With this advice in mind, Introducing Issues with Opposing Viewpoints books aim to open readers' minds to the critically divergent views that comprise our world's most important debates.

Introducing Issues with Opposing Viewpoints simplifies for students the enormous and often overwhelming mass of material now available via print and electronic media. Collected in every volume is an array of opinions that captures the essence of a particular controversy or topic. Introducing Issues with Opposing Viewpoints books embody the spirit of nineteenth-century journalist Charles A. Dana's axiom: "Fight for your opinions, but do not believe that they contain the whole truth, or the only truth." Absorbing such contrasting opinions teaches students to analyze the strength of an argument and compare it to its opposition. From this process readers can inform and strengthen their own opinions, or be exposed to new information that will change their minds. Introducing Issues with Opposing Viewpoints is a mosaic of different voices. The authors are statesmen, pundits, academics, journalists, corporations, and ordinary people who have felt compelled to share their experiences and ideas in a public forum. Their words have been collected from newspapers, journals, books, speeches, interviews, and the Internet, the fastest growing body of opinionated material in the world.

Introducing Issues with Opposing Viewpoints shares many of the well-known features of its critically acclaimed parent series, Opposing Viewpoints. The articles are presented in a pro/con format, allowing readers to absorb divergent perspectives side by side. Active reading questions preface each viewpoint, requiring the student to approach the material thoughtfully and carefully. Useful charts, graphs, and cartoons supplement each article. A thorough introduction provides readers with crucial background on an issue. An annotated bibliography points the reader toward articles, books, and Web sites that contain additional information on the topic. An appendix of organizations to contact contains a wide variety of charities, nonprofit organizations, political groups, and private enterprises that each hold a position on the issue at hand. Finally, a comprehensive index allows readers to locate content quickly and efficiently.

Introducing Issues with Opposing Viewpoints is also significantly different from Opposing Viewpoints. As the series title implies, its presentation will help introduce students to the concept of opposing viewpoints and learn to use this material to aid in critical writing and debate. The series' four-color, accessible format makes the books attractive and inviting to readers of all levels. In addition, each viewpoint has been carefully edited to maximize a reader's understanding of the content. Short but thorough viewpoints capture the essence of an argument. A substantial, thought-provoking essay question placed at the end of each viewpoint asks the student to further investigate the issues raised in the viewpoint, compare and contrast two authors' arguments, or consider how one might go about forming an opinion on the topic at hand. Each viewpoint contains sidebars that include at-a-glance information and handy statistics. A Facts About section located in the back of the book further supplies students with relevant facts and figures.

Following in the tradition of the Opposing Viewpoints series, Greenhaven Press continues to provide readers with invaluable exposure to the controversial issues that shape our world. As John Stuart Mill once wrote: "The only way in which a human being can make some approach to knowing the whole of a subject is by hearing what can be said about it by persons of every variety of opinion and studying all modes in which it can be looked at by every character of mind. No wise man ever acquired his wisdom in any mode but this." It is to this principle that Introducing Issues with Opposing Viewpoints books are dedicated.

Introduction

Oil use impacts nearly every aspect of contemporary American society. Indeed, oil is used for transportation; to grow food; and to make products as varied as heart valve transplants, plastic water bottles, and toys. As a result of its huge appetite for oil and oil-related products, America is the largest consumer of oil in the world. It consumes so much, in fact, that it cannot produce all of that oil at home. To meet its needs, it imports oil from nations rich in fossil fuels, such as Saudi Arabia, Venezuela, Canada, and Russia. But relying on foreign nations to supply the United States with its energy opens a whole host of political, economic, and social problems. Therefore, America's leaders have sought a way to reduce U.S. dependence on foreign oil by opening Alaska's Arctic National Wildlife Refuge (ANWR) to oil exploration and drilling. However, whether this would be a beneficial or harmful move for America has been a heated topic of debate for scientists, policy makers, legislators, and environmentalists for decades.

Located in northeastern Alaska, ANWR is one of the last untouched wildernesses on Earth; yet it is also believed to contain large oil reserves that could be of great use to Americans. The refuge is located in about 1.5 million acres of pristine wilderness. This untouched, wild world is home to more than 130 bird species and larger animals such as polar bears, caribou, grizzly bears, wolves, arctic foxes, whales, and other species. Environmentalists argue that drilling in ANWR would threaten the wildlife that make the region their home. In fact, in 2005 more than a thousand scientists and natural resource managers signed a letter to President George W. Bush pleading for him to protect this vibrant environmental resource. In the letter, the scientists stressed the "importance of maintaining the biological diversity and ecosystem integrity of our nation's Arctic. . . . Sacrificing this ecosystem for an insignificant supply of our nation's energy . . . does not represent balanced resource management."[1]

However, those in favor of opening the region to oil exploration claim that drilling will have a minimal impact on Arctic wildlife and ecosystems. Nature would be adequately protected, they argue, through the use of state-of-the-art drilling equipment. Gale A. Norton,

Secretary of the U.S. Department of the Interior, has acknowledged that older drilling technology has been very damaging to land and wildlife. "[But] American ingenuity has tackled this problem," says Norton. "Today, oil exploration in the Arctic occurs only in the frozen winter. Workers build roads and platforms of ice to protect the soil and vegetation. Trucks with huge tires called rolligons distribute load weights over large areas of snow to minimize the impact on the tundra below."[2] Furthermore, today's oil excavators can use satellite imaging to pinpoint exactly where they need to drill. Other technology, such as 3-D seismic data, is able to improve excavators' ability to drill wells successfully by up to 50 percent. These technologies allow fewer total wells to be drilled, preserving even more land.

Proponents of drilling claim that any environmental effects that are sustained by drilling are worth it if they help reduce America's dependence on foreign oil. Indeed, oil from foreign sources is a problem: by 2010 the United States is expected to import as much as 70 percent from foreign nations. While some of this oil comes from friendly places such as Canada and Mexico, much of it comes from Saudi Arabia and Iraq, nations with which the United States has very complicated relationships. America's oil interests in these places have made it vulnerable to terrorists such as Osama bin Laden. In fact, bin Laden said he orchestrated the attacks of September 11, 2001, and other terrorist acts, as payback for America's oil interests in Islamic holy lands. Drilling in ANWR, it is argued, would therefore help reduce America's dependence on foreign sources of oil that in turn make it vulnerable to terrorism and war. "If Congress had opened ANWR to drilling a decade ago the nation would be that much closer to lessening its dependency on foreign oil today. America cannot afford to be saying that a decade from now."[3]

However, opponents of ANWR drilling reject this argument, saying that ANWR will not help America reduce its dependence on foreign oil. One reason is that even if ANWR was opened to oil drilling tomorrow, it would take years to bring the oil to market. It is estimated that oil from ANWR would not be able to be used for at least ten years. It would take this long to explore, excavate, and drill for oil. Once the oil was recovered, it would need to be refined and transported to the lower forty-eight states. In other words, oil from ANWR is not an immediate solution to the problem of U.S. dependency on foreign oil.

Secondly, it is unclear how much oil could actually be recovered from ANWR, or whether it is enough to help America provide for its own energy needs. The U.S. Department of the Interior has estimated that ANWR contains up to 16 billion barrels of recoverable oil. But this amount is not very much when one considers that in 2007, Americans were consuming more than 21 million barrels of oil per day. Experts at the Energy Information Administration claim the amount of oil recovered from ANWR would amount to only about 0.7 percent of the world's total oil production. On the other hand, "a modest increase in the fuel economy of cars and light trucks of about 2 miles per gallon would save more than a million barrels a day—far more than is likely to be underneath the Arctic Refuge."[4]

Whether drilling in ANWR holds the answer to America's energy problems is one of many issues explored in *Introducing Issues with Opposing Viewpoints: Oil.* Readers will also consider arguments about whether the world is running out of oil, the impact developing nations have on oil consumption, whether oil use constitutes a national security threat, and whether oil should be replaced with alternative energies such as nuclear power, wind power, and biofuels. The wealth of information and perspectives provided in the article pairs will help readers come to their own conclusions about oil and how the United States should address issues surrounding its use.

Notes

1. Arctic Refuge Science, Letter to President George W. Bush, February 14, 2005. *www.savearcticrefuge.org.*
2. Gale A. Norton, "Call of the Mild," *New York Times,* March 14, 2005, p. A21.
3. Joe Bell, "Follow the Facts and Drill in ANWR," Opinioneditorials.com, November 10, 2005. *www.opinioneditorials.com.*
4. Defenders of Wildlife, "Save the Arctic! Overview." *www.save articrefuge.org.*

Chapter 1

Is the World Running Out of Oil?

Gas shortages have been experienced in countries around the world, including China.

Viewpoint 1

The World Is Running Out of Oil

Julian Darley with Amy Goodman

"All the easy oil from Saudi Arabia and . . . from the U.S. . . . is now in decline or indeed has disappeared."

In the following viewpoint Julian Darley argues that the world is running out of oil. He says we have reached a period of peak oil, or the point at which more than 50 percent of an oil reserve has been consumed and less than half remains. As a result of this oil shortage, prices increase, which can lead to an economic recession. Darley explains that once all the oil is used up, it cannot be replenished because there is only a finite amount in the ground. Darley warns that as a result of the United States' heavy dependence on oil, it will be forced to take desperate political, economic, and environmental actions that will hurt it in the long run.

Darley is the founder of the Post Carbon Institute, a think tank addressing global reliance on cheap energy. He is also the director of Global Public Media, a portal dedicated to issues surrounding peak oil production. Amy Goodman is cofounder and host of the news program *Democracy Now!*

Democracy Now! "Transcript: Has Global Oil Production Reached Maximum Capacity? A Debate on Peak Oil," April 28, 2006. Reproduced by permission.

AS YOU READ, CONSIDER THE FOLLOWING QUESTIONS:
1. In what year did U.S. oil production peak, according to the author?
2. How long ago did the two largest periods of oil creation take place, according to the author?
3. How many barrels of oil does the world use per day, according to the author?

Amy Goodman: Peak oil occurs when half of all existing oil has been pulled from the ground. Therefore, oil becomes more expensive and the economy goes into recession. Some experts believe we're at peak now, while others disagree.

We go now to a debate on the issue. We're joined in our Firehouse studio by Julian Darley, founder and director of the Post Carbon Institute and Global Public Media. He's also author of *High Noon for Natural Gas: The New Energy Crisis*, co-author of the forthcoming book, *Relocalize Now!: Getting Ready for Climate Change and the End of Cheap Oil*. . . .

FAST FACT

According to David Strahan, author of *The Last Oil Shock*, 64 of the 98 oil-producing countries in the world have passed their geologically imposed production peak. Of these, 60 are in a production decline from which they will not recover.

What Is Peak Oil?

Can you explain the concept of peak oil?

Julian Darley: Peak oil is essentially quite a simple idea. It comes about because when you have a reserve of conventional oil, either in a single reservoir or more particularly in a nation, when you get roughly halfway through, as you said, roughly halfway through that reservoir or that nation's stock, if you like, of conventional oil, then you see a decline in that oil. In other words, the production rises over a period of time—that depends partly on how much effort you put in and also, to some extent, on the geology in the reservoirs themselves—. . . .

Gas shortages may cause stations to close pumps when they run out of fuel.

When you get roughly halfway through—in fact, the world averages about 53; there's nothing magical about 50—when you get roughly halfway through, then, because of a mixture of technical, economic and geological factors in the structures of reservoirs themselves, you go into a decline. There are no exceptions to this for reservoirs, unless you apply very powerful so-called secondary and tertiary recovery techniques, which means pushing in water or carbon dioxide and things like that. Even so, you can hold some reservoirs at a plateau for a while, and then they go into decline. . . . One of the dangers is when you do that, your decline is even faster and difficult to predict.

Peak Oil Is Happening Now

Amy Goodman: And what makes you think it's happening now?

Julian Darley: Well, history has shown—the most dramatic example being that of the U.S., which its own oil production peaked in 1970—history shows that this happens to all nations. Now, when it happened to the U.S., it was able to import yet more oil. It was already an oil importer in 1970. It was able to import yet more oil. Now it imports approximately 60% and rising. So when this happens to a nation, it turns to other oil-producing nations. The trouble is when it happens to the world, and the world is roughly halfway through its conventional oil, there are no other planets to turn to to import from. So then, you get this phenomenon of global oil peak. There's no one else to import from, so the decline begins to happen.

And it does look as if we're about halfway through the conventional oil reserve of some two-and-a-bit trillion barrels. We've used a bit more than a trillion now. And so it's absolutely inevitable that it will happen. There are corroborating data from various other sources which suggest it's happening around about now. And there's some more technical data—we can go into them if you'd like. So, it's not just the fact that production figures suggest we're about halfway through, there's lots of other corroborating data, as well. . . .

Reports of Oil Grow: Oil Does Not

Julian Darley: The amount of oil in the ground simply doesn't grow. What happens is the amount of reported oil can grow, but most geologists now accept and have long admitted privately, that they know roughly what's in the ground when they make the discoveries, but it's not wise or convenient for integrated oil companies, the large oil companies, to report those early numbers. So they report a much lower amount. They're forced to by the S.E.C. [Securities and Exchange Commission] and other reporting regulations, so it makes legal sense for them to report less than they believe to be there. The nice thing about that, from their point of view, is let's say you find a billion barrels and you only report half of it—and it's perfectly legal to do so—that means next year, when you, say, don't find very much, you can report a bit more, and then the same thing the next year after that. So it's been very convenient for the oil companies, but it doesn't mean

How Oil Was Formed

Oil was formed from the remains of animals and plants that lived millions of years ago. Over the years, the remains were covered in layers of mud. Heat and pressure from these layers helped the remains turn into what we today call crude oil. The word "petroleum" means "rock oil" or "oil from the earth."

Plants and animals died and were buried in the earth. Over time, they were covered by layers of silt and sand.

Over millions of years, the remains were buried deeper and deeper. The enormous heat and pressure turned them into oil and gas.

Sand and silt

Plant and animal remains

Today, we drill down through layers of sand, silt, and rock to reach the rock formations that contain oil and gas deposits.

Sand and silt

Oil and gas deposits

the amount of oil in the ground grows, and this is very, very important. It simply doesn't.

What is there, is there from about a billion or so years of geological and plant activity. There were two large charges about 150 million years ago and about 90 million years ago, ironically from two periods of enhanced global warming. There have been several other periods, although those look like the biggest periods of deposition and creation, production of oil in the ground. That doesn't grow. What makes some difference is new technology, which has been in place for the last 20, 30, 40 years, although there is considerable evidence that even new technology doesn't really increase the recovery factor very much, at least not very much in the last 20 to 30 years. It helps you to get it out more quickly, doesn't increase that recovery factor, which varies between about 25% and 40% normally. It can be a bit higher.

So, what you're looking at is, number one, real oil that we can really get out does not grow, just the reporting of it. And now, as you see from Shell a couple of years ago, they were forced to admit that their reserves were not nearly as big as they said. Very complex issue. It's true, that this is a matter of reporting. And ultimately, it's molecules that people need to put in their cars and to feed the petrochemical industry, not just reports of molecules. . . .

The Cost of Oil Extraction Is Increasing

Julian Darley: I think it's also important to stress that, at the moment, we're not running out, it's more that we're running down, and the running down is key. When you always need more of something and you start to run down in your supply, that's absolutely critical. Running out—actual running out, i.e. no oil left in the ground, that would be a very long way off, but when you're using 85 million barrels a day and you need to increase, that becomes the issue. As to the price of getting it out, if you're referring to that, that is undoubtedly increasing, and not only the dollar price, but the energy price of getting oil and indeed other energy materials out of the ground, that's also increasing.

So, as the years go on, we will see or we will find—and it will be difficult to measure—that we will be getting less energy, as it were, for our energy buck. So that will start to have an important effect. You see the difficulties with the amount of money things cost. For instance, the tar sands in Canada, it's hard to get an exact amount of how much that costs, but certainly when you go to polar and arctic oil and gas, that is going to be really expensive. We're thinking of North Canadian gas and Russian gas. That is going to really start to show up how difficult it is, and I think it shows you how desperate we're getting that all the easy oil from Saudi Arabia and indeed from the U.S., all the cheap stuff is now in decline or indeed has disappeared in some cases, and so we really are getting pretty desperate.

EVALUATING THE AUTHORS' ARGUMENTS:

Julian Darley argues that the world is running out of oil and that global oil supplies are quickly being depleted. But the author of the following viewpoint, Max Schulz, argues that oil reserves are growing due to new detection and extraction methods. How do you account for this discrepancy? How can these authors reach such different conclusions about how much oil is left in the world? Explain your answer using evidence from the text.

The World Is Not Running Out of Oil

Max Schulz

"Even as we have been pumping more oil out of the ground, we have seen estimates of the world's proven reserves . . . grow."

The world is not running out of oil, argues Max Schulz in the following viewpoint. In fact, Schulz claims that oil reserves are growing despite the dominant belief that the world's oil is being depleted at an unprecedented rate. According to Schulz this growth is due to technological advances in the detection and extraction of oil. So much oil is waiting to be found, in fact, that Schulz believes that 82 percent of the world's oil and gas resources have yet to be consumed. Lastly, Schulz rejects the idea that the world is running out of oil, calling this a myth that has been perpetuated by supposed "experts." Rather, he concludes, history has shown that with human ingenuity and advances in technology there will be plenty of oil to meet the world's needs for hundreds of years.

Max Schulz is a senior fellow at the Center for Energy Policy and the Environment at the Manhattan Institute for Policy Research.

Max Schulz, "Energy and the Environment: Myths and Facts," *www.manhattan-institute.org*, April, 2007. Reproduced by permission.

AS YOU READ, CONSIDER THE FOLLOWING QUESTIONS:
1. The world has how many years' worth of recoverable oil resources, according to the author?
2. Proven reserves of the world's oil, gas, and natural gas liquids comprise how many barrels of oil?
3. Does the author agree with the idea that the United States is addicted to oil? Why or why not?

Common sense tells us that there is a fixed amount of oil in the earth and that each day we are getting closer to using it up. The same goes for other nonrenewable energy sources, such as coal and natural gas.

Oil Reserves Are Growing

Are we right to worry? Not anytime soon. Paradoxically, even as we have been pumping more oil out of the ground, we have seen estimates of the world's proven reserves (the amount of identified oil deposits that can be economically recovered using current technology) grow. In 1944, for instance, experts thought that the world had 51 billion barrels of crude oil left. Yet over the next six decades, we would pump more than 18 times that amount (917 billion barrels). Today, proven reserves have grown to more than 1.2 trillion barrels, a figure higher than the 1 trillion barrels that humanity has produced and consumed to date.

A Century's Worth of Oil

We have not "created" more oil. Rather, enterprising individuals have improved our technologies for detecting and extracting it. Twenty years ago, for instance, it was impossible to reach much of the oil under the deep waters of the North Sea. Now it costs less than $15 per barrel to extract it.

Taking into account new extraction technologies and discoveries of unconventional petroleum sources—which are not taken into account when calculating proven reserves—the world has at least a century's worth of recoverable oil resources. The British-based consultancy HIS Energy suggests that the planet's recoverable reserves might be as much as 2.4 trillion barrels. ExxonMobil has estimated global conventional oil resources at 3.2 trillion barrels.

Billions Left by Other Counts

Unconventional sources, such as oil shale deposits in the western United States and the oil sands in Canada and Venezuela, will yield even more recoverable resources. ExxonMobil's recent estimates suggest that there are 800,000 billion barrels of recoverable oil from these sources. Petro-Canada is more optimistic, estimating that Canada by itself has "more than 2.5 trillion barrels [in unconventional oil resources]. These deposits rival those of the Middle East and could satisfy today's global demand for the next 100 years."

These estimates may be conservative. As *Reason* magazine science correspondent Ronald Bailey notes, the U.S. Geological Survey "figures that the total world endowment of conventional oil resources is equivalent to about 5.9 trillion barrels of oil. *Proven* reserves of oil, gas, and natural gas liquids are equivalent to 2 trillion barrels of oil. The USGS calculates that humanity has already consumed about 1 trillion barrels of oil equivalent, which means 82 percent of the world's endowment of oil and gas resources remains to be used."

> **FAST FACT**
>
> Fears that oil will run out have endured for centuries. In 1874, for example, the state geologist of Pennsylvania warned the government that the United States had only enough oil to last for four years.

We Are Not Headed Toward a Global Catastrophe

It is important to note, too, that experts have repeatedly provided dire warnings about our running out of oil. The preeminent proponent of this school of thought was geologist Marion King Hubbert, who predicted in the 1950s that world oil production would peak around the year 2000. In other words, according to the "Hubbert's Peak" theory, we have passed the halfway point in terms of the world's recoverable oil production. A number of present-day oil-industry observers have taken up Hubbert's idea and believe that we are heading toward global economic catastrophe. If the world has used up about half its oil in about a century, goes the argument, what does that imply for the twenty-first century, given the increased demand for oil in China, India, and the developing world?

The good news about this bad news is that, historically, the doomsayers have been wrong. If the past is prologue to our future, technology and human ingenuity will likely prove today's doomsayers wrong as well. . . .

America Is Not Addicted to Oil

In perhaps the most memorable line of his 2006 State of the Union address, President Bush announced that "America is addicted to oil."

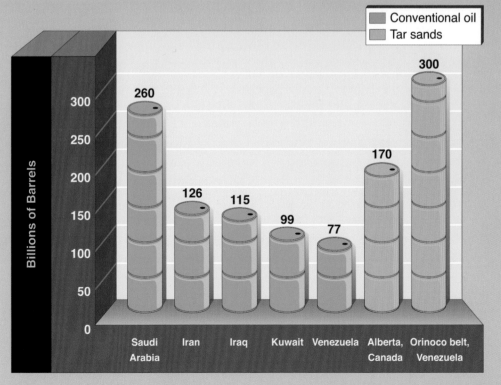

Billions of Barrels Exist in Nontraditional Sources

The world's reserves of oil found in nontraditional sources, such as shale rock and tar sand, are immense. Some believe these reserves even exceed the reserves of conventional oil and natural gas. Most of these reserves have yet to be tapped.

Legend:
- Conventional oil
- Tar sands

Billions of Barrels

Source	Billions of Barrels
Saudi Arabia	260
Iran	126
Iraq	115
Kuwait	99
Venezuela	77
Alberta, Canada	170
Orinoco belt, Venezuela	300

Taken from: *Oil & Gas Journal.*

The line was as notable for its frankness as for the fact that it was uttered by a former oil-industry executive. The president proposed a host of alternative-energy research programs to deal with this dependency. Eighty-three percent of initial survey respondents agreed with the president's assessment of the nation's energy situation. In the wake of the president's 2007 State of the Union address, in which he repeated several themes from his 2006 speech, the percentage of respondents believing that our nation is addicted to oil was virtually unchanged (84 percent). But is that assessment correct?

[In actuality,] oil is a much less dominant player in our energy economy than most people think. It does not even provide the majority of the energy that we use, supplying 40 percent of energy consumption. The rest of the energy economy—60 percent—is accounted for by sources that, for the most part, provide electricity: coal, natural gas, nuclear power, and renewable energies such as hydropower, biomass, wind, and solar. Given the diversity that defines the American energy economy, it is misleading to say that the United States is "addicted" to oil. . . .

Americans Do Not Understand Energy Issues

Despite the importance of energy in our daily lives and the media attention that energy and environmental issues generate, the survey results show that Americans are often misinformed about basic energy issues. We are not running out of energy. Our "dependence" on foreign energy is not the Achilles' heel that many would have us believe. . . .

Why don't we know more about energy? Perhaps because, for the most part, we've rarely had to worry about it. As United States secretary of energy Samuel Bodman remarked in a 2005 speech to the Electric Power Association, "The energy we use is so constant, so dependable, so reliable, and—in relative terms—so affordable that consumers not only don't give it a second thought, they hardly give it a first one either."

Energy topics are not easy to contemplate. They can be highly technical and seem overly complicated. Moreover, energy and environmental issues treat a wide spectrum of somewhat unrelated topics, ranging from thermodynamics and agriculture to species protection and underground mining to foreign affairs and religion. Add to this the fact that in our advanced economy, the vast major-

Some people believe that new technologies, like extracting oil from shale, will prevent the world from running out of oil in the near future.

ity of consumption is hidden from view, and it's no wonder that the average consumer is ignorant of the details of energy production. Consumers have long assumed that flipping the switch means that the light goes on, but few stop to think about the energy economy beyond the wall socket that makes it all possible. Given the constancy and reliability alluded to by Secretary Bodman, there's little reason that they should.

Misunderstanding Energy Issues Is Dangerous

Yet, whatever the reason for our ignorance, it is dangerous. The wide disconnect between what the public believes about energy issues and what is actually true has already moved our policies in unwise directions: . . .

- Our belief that America's oil use is inherently harmful has led us to adopt a number of failed policies. In 1980, the Carter administration set up the Synthetic Fuels Corporation to devise alternatives to crude oil. The program lost tens of billions of dollars with no success. Policymakers have also promoted ethanol as a substitute for gasoline, going so far in the 2005 Energy Policy Act as to mandate the use of 7.5 billion gallons of ethanol in the U.S. energy supply by 2012. This mandate comes on top of the several billion dollars in subsidies that the federal and state governments provide to ethanol R&D [research and development] and production each year, subsidies that have done virtually nothing to increase ethanol's share in our energy mix.

- The belief that we are running out of oil, like the belief that we are addicted to oil, has pushed federal R&D efforts into a number of areas that have cost taxpayers vast sums of money but failed (as of yet) to yield any tangible results. The federal government has long invested in creating vehicles to run on fuels other than gasoline and vehicles far more efficient than current models. The Clinton administration started the Partnership for a New Generation of Vehicles (PNGV) to develop vehicles capable of getting 80 miles to the gallon. That program was replaced by the Bush administration's similar FreedomCAR program. President Bush also introduced a multibillion-dollar federal program to work with automakers and energy companies in developing hydrogen fuel cell technologies, with the idea of displacing the internal combustion engine. Meanwhile, the federal government has long mandated Corporate Average Fuel Economy standards for automotive vehicle fleets. Critics have noted that these standards have led automakers to produce lighter, less-crashworthy cars. . . .

Let the Market Dictate Our Energy Future

Our energy and environmental policies must center on the best proven mechanism for finding solutions to our future challenges. The process of moving beyond a petroleum-based economy is happening not because of government targets or imperial dictates but because that is the direction that free markets appear to be leading us. Market forces are spurring the electrification of the economy. Whereas several generations ago, we relied on petroleum for much of our electricity, today we depend on nuclear power and natural gas for that share, an evolution shaped by economic realities. Whereas today our transportation sector relies almost exclusively on oil, tomorrow we can expect to depend to a much larger degree on electricity and, by extension, coal, uranium, natural gas, and renewable energy.

EVALUATING THE AUTHOR'S ARGUMENTS:

In this viewpoint the author presents several different estimates of how much oil is left in the world. Why do the numbers vary? What factors affect these estimates? Do you think it matters who or what organization has given these estimates? Explain your reasoning and support your answer with evidence from the text.

Oil Shortages Are Manufactured by Oil Companies

Paul Joseph Watson and Alex Jones

"Peak oil is a theory advanced by the elite, by the oil industry, by the very people that you would think peak oil would harm."

In the following viewpoint Paul Joseph Watson and Alex Jones argue that oil shortages are fabricated by the oil industry to jack up the cost of fossil fuels. Watson and Jones explain that when oil companies report shortages, it allows them to raise prices because there is more demand for oil than supply. But such shortages are artificial, the authors claim. In actuality, new sources of oil are being discovered everywhere on Earth and some evidence even suggests that oil may actually be replenishing itself. As a result, oil reserves are increasing daily, and the rate of production is continuing to rise, which contradicts the popular notion that the world is running out of oil. Watson and Jones conclude that oil shortages are a myth created to make consumers and the economy dependent on oil, which only serves to increase the profits of oil companies.

Watson is a regular contributor to Prison Planet.com, a liberal activist Web site. Jones is the founder and creator of PrisonPlanet.com as well as a radio host and filmmaker.

Paul Joseph Watson and Alex Jones, "The Myth of Peak Oil," *PrisonPlanet.com*, October 12, 2005. Reproduced by permission.

AS YOU READ, CONSIDER THE FOLLOWING QUESTIONS:
1. According to the most recent estimates, how many barrels of oil are likely contained within probable reserves, as reported by Watson and Jones?
2. What country has surpassed Saudi Arabia's oil reserves, according to the authors?
3. Russians have pumped money into what type of oil excavation, according to the authors?

P eak oil is a scam designed to create artificial scarcity and jack up prices while giving the state an excuse to invade our lives and order us to sacrifice our hard-earned living standards. . . .

Peak oil is a theory advanced by the elite, by the oil industry, by the very people that you would think peak oil would harm, unless it was a cover for another agenda. Which from the evidence of artificial scarcity being deliberately created, the reasons for doing so and who benefits, it's clear that peak oil is a myth and it should be exposed for what it is. Another excuse for the Globalists to seize more control over our lives and sacrifice more American sovereignty in the meantime.

The Lies of Artificial Scarcity

The crux of the issue is that if oil was plentiful in areas in which we are being told by the government and the oil companies that it is not, then we have clear evidence that artificial scarcity is being simulated in order to drive forward a myriad of other agendas. And we have concrete examples of where this has happened.

Three separate internal confidential memos from Mobil, Chevron and Texaco have been obtained by The Foundation for Taxpayer and Consumer Rights. These memos outline a deliberate agenda to gouge prices and create artificial scarcity by limiting capacities of and outright closing oil refineries. This was a nationwide lobbying effort led by the American Petroleum Institute [API] to encourage refineries to do this.

An internal Chevron memo states; "A senior energy analyst at the recent API convention warned that if the US petroleum industry doesn't reduce its refining capacity it will never see any substantial increase in refinery margins."

High crude oil prices benefit companies like ExxonMobil, allowing them to become the U.S. company with the largest annual profit.

The memos make clear that blockages in refining capacity and opening new refineries did not come from environmental organizations, as the oil industry claimed, but via a deliberate policy of limitation and price gouging at the behest of the oil industry itself.

Oil Can Naturally Replenish Itself

Eugene Island is an oil field in the gulf of Mexico, 80 miles off the coast of Louisiana. It was discovered in 1973 and began producing 15,000 barrels of oil a day which then slowed to about 4,000 barrels in 1989. But then for no logical reason whatsoever, production spiked back up to 13,000 barrels a day.

What the researchers found when they analyzed the oil field with time lapse 3-D seismic imaging is that there was an unexplained deep fault in the bottom corner of the computer scan, which showed oil gushing in from a previously unknown deep source and migrating up through the rock to replenish the existing supply.

Furthermore, the analysis of the oil now being produced at Eugene Island shows that its age is geologically different from the oil produced there after the refinery first opened. Suggesting strongly that it is now emerging from a different, unexplained source.

The last estimates of probable reserves shot up from 60 million barrels to 400 million barrels. Both the scientists and geologists from the big oil companies have seen the evidence and admitted that the Eugene Island oil field is refilling itself.

This completely contradicts peak oil theory and with technology improving at an accelerating pace it seems obvious that there are more Eugene Islands out there waiting to be discovered. So the scientific community needs to embrace these possibilities and lobby for funding into finding more of these deep source replenishing oil fields.

The existence of self-renewing oil fields shatters the peak oil myth. If oil is a naturally replenishing inorganic substance then how can it possibly run out?

"Oil Is Secure and Plentiful"

This year in particular we have seen a strong hike in oil prices and are being told to simply get used to it because this is the way it is going to be. In the wake of Hurricanes Katrina and Rita [in 2005] gas prices have shot up amid claims of vast energy shortages. Americans

> **FAST FACT**
>
> As of January 1, 2006, proven oil reserves amounted to about 1,293 billion barrels. One barrel equals 42 gallons, or 159 liters.

are being asked to turn off lights, change thermostat settings, drive slower, insulate homes and take other steps. Meanwhile the oil companies continue to make record profits.

Flying in the face of the so called peak oil crisis are the facts. If we are running out of oil so quickly then why are reserves being continually increased and production skyrocketing?

In the 1980s OPEC decided to switch to a quota production system based on the size of reserves. The larger the reserves a country said it had the more it could pump.

Earlier this year Saudi Arabia reportedly increased its crude reserves by around 200 billion barrels. Saudi oil is secure and plentiful, say officials. "These huge reserves enable the Kingdom to remain a major oil producer for between 70 and 100 years, even if it raises its production capacity to 15 million barrels per day, which may well happen during the next 15 years."

Is this the normal course of behavior if we are currently at the peak for oil production? The answer is no, it's the normal course of action for increasing production.

New Oil Sources Are Discovered Everywhere

There have also been reports that Russia has vastly increased its reserves even beyond those of Saudi Arabia. Why would they do this if they believed there would be no more oil to get hold of? It seems clear that Russia is ready for unlimited future production of oil.

There is a clear contradiction between the peak oil theory and the continual increase in oil reserves and production. New untapped oil sources are being discovered everywhere on earth. The notion that there are somehow only a few sources that the West is trying to monopolize is a complete myth, promulgated by those raking in the massive profits. After all how do you make huge profits from something available in abundance?

Oil Prices Remain High

A *Wall Street Journal* article by Peter Huber and Mark Mills describes how the price of oil remains high because the cost of oil remains so low. We are not dependent on the middle east for oil because the world's supplies are diminishing, it is because it is more profitable to tap middle east supplies. Thus the myth of peak oil is needed in order to silence the call for tapping the planet's other plentiful reserves.

[Entrepreneur] Richard Branson has even stated his intention to set up his own refinery because the price of oil is artificially being kept high whilst new sources are not being explored and new refineries not being built. "Opec is effectively an illegal cartel that can meet happily, nobody takes them to court," Branson has said. "They collude to keep prices high."

So if more refineries were built and different resources tapped, the oil prices would come down and the illegal cartel OPEC would see profits diminish. It is no wonder then that the argument for peak oil is so appealing to OPEC. If no one invests to build refineries because they don't believe there is enough oil, then who benefits? OPEC and the oil elites of course.

Is Demand for Oil Decreasing?

It seems that every time there is some kind of energy crisis, OPEC increases production. The remarkable thing about this is that they always state that they are doing it to ease prices, yet prices always shoot up because they promulgate the myth that they are putting some of their last reserves into the market. Analysts seem confused and always state that they don't believe upping production will cut prices.

History of Oil Shocks: 1970–2005

The price of oil tends to ebb and flow in relation to political events.

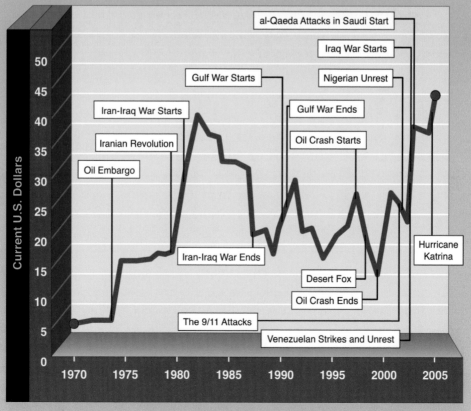

Taken from: EIA, "Crude Prices by Selected Type, 1970–2005," available at: www.eia.doe.gov/emeu/aer/txt/ptb1107.html.

In a recent report the International Monetary Fund [IMF] projected that global demand for oil by 2030 would reach 139 million barrels a day, a 65 percent increase. "We should expect to live with high and volatile oil prices," said Raghuram Rajan, the IMF's chief economist. "In short, it's going to be a rocky road going forward."

Yet independent analysts and even some within OPEC seem to believe that the demand for oil is diminishing. Why the contradiction?

The peak oil and demand myth is peddled by the establishment-run fake left activist groups, OPEC and globalist arms such as the IMF. *Rolling Stone* magazine even carried an article in its April [2005] issue heavily biased towards making people believe the peak oil lie.

The scientific evidence also flies in the face of the peak oil theory. Scientific research dating back over a hundred years, more recently updated in a scientific paper published in *Energia* suggests that oil is abiotic, not the product of long decayed biological matter. Oil, for better or for worse, is not a non-renewable resource. It, like coal, and natural gas, replenishes from sources within the mantle of earth.

No coincidence then that the Russians, who pioneered this research have pumped expenditure into deep underground oil excavation. . . .

If we continue to let the corrupt elite tell us we are wholly dependent on oil, we may reach a twisted situation whereby they can justify starvation and mass global poverty, perhaps even depopulation, even within the western world due to the fact that our energy supplies are finished.

Peak oil is just another weapon the globalists have in their arsenal to move towards a new world order where the elite get richer and everyone else falls into line.

EVALUATING THE AUTHORS' ARGUMENTS:

In this viewpoint the author argues that oil companies manufacture oil shortages in order to increase their profits. How do you think each of the other authors in this chapter might respond to this suggestion? List each speaker and write two to three sentences on what you think their response might be.

Oil Shortages Are a Real Threat

Paul Phillips

"Civilization as we know it will come to an end some time in this century, when the fuel runs out."

In the following viewpoint author Paul Phillips claims that oil shortages are a real threat and warns that the world is on the brink of experiencing an energy crisis. The United States is at particular risk because it depends on oil more than any other nation in the world. America has the highest per capita oil consumption, he explains, and must therefore encroach on world supplies to meet its energy needs. Phillips concludes that America's rate of oil use cannot be sustained over the long run and warns that it is unlikely to retain its global influence unless it changes its energy policy and addresses the seriousness of the situation.

Phillips is a contributor to *Canadian Dimension*, a leftist magazine from which this viewpoint was taken.

AS YOU READ, CONSIDER THE FOLLOWING QUESTIONS:
1. What does the author mean when he discusses "petroleum ghost slaves"?
2. How much of the world's petroleum reserves does Phillips say have been identified?
3. How many barrels of water does it take to produce one barrel of oil? What bearing does this have on the author's argument?

Paul Phillips, "The American Empire Meets Peak Oil," *Canadian Dimension*, January/February 2006. Reproduced by permission of the author.

W hile Canada's economic elite continues to push further integration into the American economic empire, it seems blissfully ignorant of the fact that globalization, the American Empire, is a falling star that is simply running out of gas.

The reason is "peak oil," the peaking and future decline in supplies of crude oil. The American economy is not only based on oil, it is totally dependent on it. As North American oil supplies decline, the American Empire must expand, by force if necessary, to incorporate more and more of the world's dwindling petroleum sources within its economic control.

Fossil Fuels and Empire

The British Empire's expansion was fueled by cheap coal. By the 1850s England had become the "workshop of the world," and proceeded to impose "free trade imperialism" on much of the rest of the world. But imperial overreach, war and technological change—the move from coal to oil—brought an end to the British Empire and, with it, a period of "de-globalization."

As for the U.S.—fueled by its own supply of cheap oil, aided by the Bretton Woods financial institutions (the IMF, World Bank and GATT/WTO)—its empire began to expand after the Second World War. Following the Soviet collapse in 1989, the U.S.'s economic empire was left without any effective constraints except two: global warming and peak oil.

Oil Supplies Are Declining

Fossil-fuel industrialism produces global-warming gases. Only recently have we have begun to realize how much these temperature-increasing gases threaten not only the global economy and ecology, but all human life on this planet. While the world (except the United States) has woken up to the threat of global warming, it has not seen the possibility that the problem may be self-correcting. Simply put, world oil supplies are peaking and will soon begin to decline. But that is like saying we don't have to worry about dying of cancer, because we will die of heart disease first.

[American journalist] Richard Heinberg, in an article entitled "Oil, War and Terror," describes the problem graphically: "The industrial

Who Consumes the Most Oil?

Consuming about 20.8 million barrels per day, the United States uses the most oil in the world.

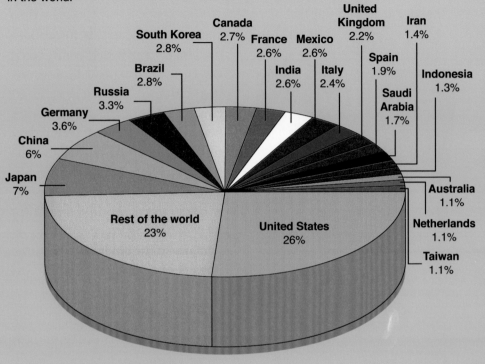

Taken from: Public Broadcasting Service, 2007.

revolution, still continuing, is all about replacing human and animal labor with the work of machines running directly or indirectly on fossil energy. Each day, the energy from oil used by people around the world equals the work of some 180 billion humans. It is as if the average global man, woman, or child had 30 slaves toiling around the clock. But those petroleum 'ghost slaves' are not evenly distributed. Each of us in the U.S. has, on average, more than 120 of them. This is the energetic basis of our American Way of Life." What happens when these "slaves" die?

Emerging Oil Crisis

In 1956 oil-company geologist King Hubbert forecast that, approximately 20 years after American oilfields began production, their output would begin to decline, following a typical "bell curve" pattern. Though ridiculed at the time, his prediction for the U.S. proved absolutely accurate. In 1970 output began to decline. A similar pattern has occurred in Canadian production of conventional crude. At the world level, supplies of conventional crude can be expected to begin declining approximately two decades after new discoveries reach their maximum, and this is now happening. Already it is estimated that 98 per cent of the world's petroleum reserves have been identified, so "new" oil potential is virtually non-existent.

While world supply is increasingly constrained, world demand for oil is increasing exponentially, particularly in the emerging industrial powers of China and India. This means that the price of oil is unlikely to fall much from its current, elevated level and should, in the longer run, increase much more. Shifting to heavy oils, oil sands and oil shales will increase supply only temporarily, and at much higher cost, both in money and in energy inputs.

Already, Goldman Sachs has predicted oil prices spiking to U.S. $105 per barrel in the near future, though they do concede that, if the spike shocks American consumers into trading in their SUVs for hybrids and compact cars and to begin conserving energy, the price of crude could fall back temporarily, which happened after the oil crisis of the early 1970s.

Oil Production Is Falling

Conditions in 2005, however, are very different than those in the 1980s. The major difference is that there no longer exists a significant excess pumping capacity anywhere in the world. Indeed, for many countries and oilfields, including Canada, the U.S., Mexico, Venezuela and the North Sea, production of conventional crude is falling. Matt Simmons, an investment banker, energy specialist and author of *Twilight in the Desert: The Coming Saudi Oil Shock and the World Economy*, has suggested that Saudi Arabia's Ghawar field, the world's largest, has already plateaued, and, given its very high pumping rate, risks imminent collapse. To make matters worse, U.S. production of natural gas, the best alternative fuel for heating and electricity generation, is also falling, while Canadian supplies are peaking. The alternative—liquid natural gas from offshore—is both expensive and dangerous.

We won't know if we have reached the global oil peak until after it occurs, but most forecasts estimate it will occur between 2005 and 2010. Even the most optimistic are unwilling to push the peak beyond about 2020. Almost all agree that it's not if, but when, world oil production will begin to fall. And when it does, real energy prices will begin to escalate. Ali Bakhtiar, the Iranian creator of the World Oil Production Capacity model, warns that prices could reach $125 per barrel by 2006 even before his predicted 2008 oil peak. . . .

The United States' dependency on petroleum permeates all aspects of life, including the fuel that powers cars, generates electricity, and heats homes.

The End of Civilization

Petroleum powers much of the world's manufacturing activity, including plastics, pharmaceuticals, agricultural chemicals and fertilizers. Further, not only does it fuel manufacturing, it smelts and refines our metals, generates electricity, heats and cools our homes and offices, and—perhaps most importantly—fills the tanks of our gas-guzzling vehicles. As Dr. David Goodstein notes in his article, "Running Out of Gas," "Our vehicles, our roads, our cities, our power plants, our entire social organization has evolved on the promise of an endless supply of cheap oil." Dramatically, he concludes: "Civilization as we know it will come to an end some time in this century, when the fuel runs out."

Alternative Oil Also Has Limits

Politicians have blissfully ignored the impending peak-oil crisis. Indeed, many governments in Canada have gleefully anticipated higher oil prices hoping to grease their provincial economies—particularly Alberta, which stands to gain from rising oil and gas prices in the medium run. However, even Alberta's supplies of conventional oil are already declining, and, though spiraling crude prices have spurred production of synthetic oil, it comes at a heavy cost in pollution, water consumption and energy use. (The French firm Total has been exploring the idea of building a nuclear plant to provide the required energy.) In the longer run, synthetic oil, too, will be subject to its own peak.

Canadian industry is more aware than governments of the tar sands' limits. Writing in *Canadian Business*, Andrew Nikiforuk observed that, "Like most big energy projects, Alberta's oilsands will deliver more hyperbole than oil . . . the ever-prudent BP Statistical Review lists only 16.9 billion barrels as recoverable and under active development." Higher estimates "just don't reflect economic, environmental and engineering constraints." They also ignore that synthetic crude production uses enormous amounts of natural gas and that "the burning of gas to make oil [is] a process akin to turning gold into lead." Furthermore, it takes about 1.5 barrels of water—a resource of which Alberta is already short—to produce one barrel of oil.

Warnings Unheeded

Meanwhile, the United States is developing its own energy policy, with horrendous global implications. The Bush Administration has received numerous reports on peak oil and the threat it poses to the "American way of life" from academic, military and private sources. As early as April, 2001, the U.S. Council on Foreign Relations reported to [President George W.] Bush that, "As the 21st century opens, the energy sector is in critical condition. . . . The world is currently close to utilizing all of its available global oil production capacity, raising the chances of an oil supply crisis with more substantial consequences than seen in three decades."

But rather than attempting to reduce consumption, conserve oil and develop alternatives, the U.S. has been expanding its empire to capture control of remaining world supplies. When asked what America's energy policy was, the *Weekly Standard*'s Irwin Stelzer reportedly replied, "Aircraft carriers." The wars in Afghanistan, Iraq, Colombia and Yugoslavia; the war being planned against Iran; the attempted coup in Venezuela; regime changes orchestrated and/or attempted in Georgia, Ukraine, North Korea and Lebanon; and the rearming of Japan and establishment of military bases throughout southeast Asia and eastern Europe have all been tied to the U.S.'s search for control of the world's remaining oil supplies.

"The American Way of Life"

Control of oil is critical to the U.S. because globalization, the American Empire, the U.S. economy and the American way of life all depend on oil. U.S. per-capita consumption is approximately 25 barrels per year—double that of western Europe, more than five times the world average and 16 times higher than that of China. The U.S. produces only a third of the oil it consumes, so that its dependence upon imports was rising even before the hurricanes further reduced domestic supplies. And maintaining an empire is very expensive and energy-intensive.

EVALUATING THE AUTHOR'S ARGUMENTS:

In this viewpoint the author, Paul Phillips, quotes from several sources to support the points he makes in his essay. Make a list of everyone he quotes, including their credentials and the nature of their comments. Then, analyze his sources—are they credible? Are they well qualified to speak on the subject?

Growing Demand in Developing Nations Will Make Oil Run Out Faster

Jehangir Pocha

"'There is just not enough oil in the world' to cover China's and India's growing energy needs."

In the following viewpoint Jehangir Pocha warns that growing demand for oil in developing nations like China and India is depleting the world's oil supply at breakneck speed. He explains how the Chinese and Indian economies are industrializing at a rapid pace, requiring them to consume more and more oil to meet their energy needs. As the standard of living in these countries is raised, more people will drive cars or obtain other devices that are powered by fossil fuels. The author is worried about this development, because world demand for oil is already straining world supplies—adding the demand of developing nations is likely to tip the scales. According to Pocha the relationship between these new world players will

Jehangir Pocha, "The Axis of Oil," *In These Times*, January 31, 2005. Reproduced by permission of the publisher, www.inthesetimes.com.

likely clash with the United States as each vies to secure whatever oil remains on Earth.

Pocha is the Asia correspondent for *In These Times*, a magazine dedicated to providing a forum for social, environmental, and economic justice discussions, and from which this viewpoint is taken.

AS YOU READ, CONSIDER THE FOLLOWING QUESTIONS:
1. In what year will China have more cars than the United States, according to the author?
2. As reported by the author how many million barrels a day does India currently consume? How many will it consume by 2025?
3. What country signed a deal with Venezuela and Colombia in 2004 to construct a pipeline between those two countries?

China and India are locked in an increasingly aggressive wrangle with the United States over the world's most critical economic commodity: oil. More than any other issue, this tussle will shape the economic, environmental and geopolitical future of these three countries, and the world.

The U.S. Faces Competition for Oil

Ensuring a steady flow of cheap oil has always been one of the central goals of U.S. foreign and economic policy, and Washington's preeminent position in the world is based in large measure on its ability to do this. But China and India are increasingly competing with the United States to secure oil exploration rights in Africa, Southeast Asia, Central Asia and Latin America.

[As of February 2005] India has invested more than $3 billion in global exploration ventures and has said it will continue to spend $3 billion a year on more acquisitions. China, which has already invested about $15 billion in foreign oil fields, is expected to spend lots more over the next decade.

The motive, says Zheng Hongfei, an energy researcher at the Beijing Institute of Technology, is that "there is just not enough oil in the world" to cover China's and India's growing energy needs.

More Vehicles Require More Oil

By 2010 India will have 36 times more cars than it did in 1990. China will have 90 times more, and by 2030 it will have more cars than the United States, according to the Energy Research Institute of Beijing.

More than 4.5 million new vehicles are expected to hit Chinese roads this year alone, a far cry from the time when families saved for months to buy a Flying Pigeon bicycle. The country is now the world's largest oil importer after the United States, guzzling about 6.5 million barrels of oil a day; this figure will double by 2020, says Stephen Roach, chief economist at Morgan Stanley.

India, the world's second-fastest growing economy after China, now consumes about 2.2 million barrels a day—about the same as South Korea—and this is expected to rise to 5.3 million barrels a day by 2025, according to the U.S. Energy Information Administration.

The number of vehicles in India is growing so quickly that the infrastructure cannot keep up with road repair, provide enough parking, or manage traffic volume.

Global Demand Will Deplete Oil Reserves

With global oil production barely 1 million barrels over the global consumption rate of 81 million barrels a day, the surge in demand from China and India could eventually lead global demand to outstrip supply, causing fuel prices to shoot up beyond their recent [late 2004] highs of around $56 a barrel, says Roach. [The price of oil hit $100 per barrel in January 2008.]

The impact of this on the global economy, particularly in developing countries that import most of their fuel, would be severe. The International Energy Agency says that for every $1 increase in oil price, the global economy loses $25 billion.

Oil Reserves Affect the Global Economy

Anxiety over this is already throwing the nervous oil market into further disequilibrium. In September [2004], Michael Rothman, a senior energy analyst at Merrill Lynch, said rising oil prices were not so much a result of the Iraq war or political instability in Venezuela and Sudan, but of extensive "hoarding" by China.

According to Rothman's analysis, China and India are roiling oil markets by creating oil reserves, which are designed to provide the minimum cache the country needs to ride out a crisis, along the lines of the United States' Strategic Petroleum Reserve (SPR).

With both countries flush with foreign exchange reserves that are threatening to infect their economies with inflation, creating an oil stock seems a sensible solution. But critics say Beijing's and New Delhi's timing is unfortunate, coming just as the global economy seemed to be recovering and the United States was questioning the value of its own reserve.

At 175 million barrels and 25 million barrels respectively, China's and India's estimated oil reserves are just a small fraction of the 700 million barrels held by the United States in its SPR.

World Demand for Oil Is Increasing

Each year, developing nations add to the demand for oil. By 2025 China, India, and the rest of Asia are expected to nearly triple their oil consumption. Russia, Africa, and the Middle East will increase oil use by 60 percent, and the United States will increase by almost 40 percent.

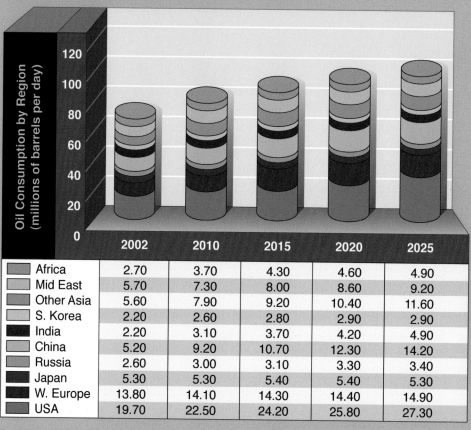

	2002	2010	2015	2020	2025
Africa	2.70	3.70	4.30	4.60	4.90
Mid East	5.70	7.30	8.00	8.60	9.20
Other Asia	5.60	7.90	9.20	10.40	11.60
S. Korea	2.20	2.60	2.80	2.90	2.90
India	2.20	3.10	3.70	4.20	4.90
China	5.20	9.20	10.70	12.30	14.20
Russia	2.60	3.00	3.10	3.30	3.40
Japan	5.30	5.30	5.40	5.40	5.30
W. Europe	13.80	14.10	14.30	14.40	14.90
USA	19.70	22.50	24.20	25.80	27.30

Oil Consumption by Region (millions of barrels per day)

Taken from: EIA, IEO2005, reference case projection.

Military and Political Support in Exchange for Oil

China and India, which are both nuclear states, are also taking advantage of the United States' strained ties with Iran, Vietnam and Myanmar by extending these countries military and political support in exchange for energy supplies. And a Washington preoccupied with Iraq, the war on terror and nuclear crises in Iran and North Korea has been unable to checkmate either country as successfully as it did earlier.

For example, U.S. nervousness over China's intentions in Latin America had led it to use its leverage with Panama to impede China's access to the all-important canal connecting the Pacific and Atlantic. But in December [2004], Beijing signed a landmark deal with Venezuela and its neighbor Colombia, under whose terms a pipeline would be constructed linking Venezuelan oil fields to ports along Colombia's Pacific coastline.

This will allow Venezuelan oil to bypass the Panama Canal and create a new and direct route to China.

Engaging in "Aggressive Oil Politics"

There are also signs that China is warming to the idea of a Russia-China-India axis, which, in cooperation with Iran, would turn the oil-rich Central Asian region into their domain. This proposal would put in place extensive military agreements and pipeline networks. Originally put forward by Russia's Asia-centric ex-Prime Minister Yevgeny Primakov, the proposal seems to be gaining ground with all four nations. China and India have already signed multibillion-dollar gas and energy deals with Russia, which is the largest arms supplier to both countries, and with ex-Soviet Central Asian republics such as Kazakhstan.

What worries Western powers most are China's and India's growing ties with Iran, a country Washington is trying to isolate. Both Beijing and New Delhi have recently signed 25-year gas and oil deals with Iran that are collectively valued at between $150 and $200 billion, and both countries are also deepening their military cooperation with Tehran. Iran and India conducted their first-ever joint naval exercises last September [2004], and India has agreed to modernize Iran's aging Russian-built Kilo-class submarines and MiG fighters.

Both China and India have also tried to thwart Western attempts to curtail Iran's nuclear program, which has largely been built with Russian assistance. In a departure from China's traditional neutrality on international issues that do not involve its own interests, Chinese Foreign Minister Li Zhaoxing flew to Tehran last November [2004] when the United States threatened to haul Iran before the U.N. Security Council and announced that China would oppose any such effort. And in January [2005], the State Department imposed penalties against some of China's largest weapons manufacturers for their support of Iran's ballistic missile program.

The potential volatility from such aggressive oil politics could bring China and India into conflict with Western, Japanese and other regional interests.

EVALUATING THE AUTHORS' ARGUMENTS:

In this viewpoint Jehangir Pocha argues that increased oil demand in developing nations is dangerously taxing the world's oil supply. In the following viewpoint author George Giles argues that the world's oil supply can handle an increase in demand. After reading both viewpoints, with which author do you agree? Explain your reasoning.

The World's Oil Supply Can Handle an Increase in Demand

George Giles

"Every year there are more proven [oil] reserves at the end of the year than at the beginning."

In the following viewpoint George Giles claims that the world contains plenty of oil, and increased demand from developing nations is not likely to deplete resources. According to Giles, the natural production theory of oil—which is the dominant theory accepted by most scientists—grossly underestimates the amount of oil in the Earth. Instead, Giles supports an alternative theory that suggests that oil pools are not being depleted and are in fact being replenished—which would explain why some large oil fields do not seem to run dry. This would also account for why, historically, there are always more proven oil reserves at the end of the year versus at the beginning. Thus the world's oil supply is not in as dire condition as politicians and leaders would like people to believe, and can handle increased demand from developing nations such as India and China.

George Giles, "The World's Oil Supply Can Handle an Increase in Demand," *LewRockwell.com*, July 6, 2006. Reproduced by permission of the publisher and author.

Giles is an independent thinker and writer in Nashville, Tennessee. He is a frequent contributor to LewRockwell.com, a Web site devoted to news and commentary.

AS YOU READ, CONSIDER THE FOLLOWING QUESTIONS:
1. If just 0.001 percent of Earth's crust has oil, how many barrels does the author say could be left?
2. Who is Freeman Dyson, and why does the author mention him?
3. According to the author what did a $25 million dollar drilling experiment in Sweden reveal about the origins of oil?

The concept of Peak Oil is that the planet is running out of a precious non-renewable natural resource and that the future will be grave if dramatic action is not forthcoming by the powers that be. All the oil that Earth has was created millions of years ago and these reservoirs are slowly, and inexorably being drained. The future will be one of increasing prices, lower supply and international conflict as industrialized and industrializing nations consume what is left. These are all unproven assertions, opinions really, they are not factual.

According to oil industry, sources, the commonly accepted proven reserves are 1.226 trillion barrels of oil. Just how much is this? Using established standards for volume the reserves in barrels of oil can be converted into cubic miles. The number that is calculated using these—about 48 cubic miles of oil. Given that the volume of the earth is much, much larger (by many billions of cubic miles), then this is really not that much oil relative to the volume of the Earth. These calculations would seem to indicate real scarcity. The world is consuming a lot of oil, and that consumption grows each and every year, the key question becomes how long until we run out? My calculations (2006) indicated this to be about 49 years at current consumption rates. This could actually be too low and thus the reserves could be dwindling faster than that depending on rates of consumption in rapidly growing economies like India and China.

The flaw in this argument is that every year there are more proven reserves at the end of the year than at the beginning, thanks to vigorous exploration and improved extraction technologies. Additionally productivity increases are found each and every year in this capital intensive industry. This has been the consistent theme for as long as oil reserves have been calculated. There has never been a time that the oil industry has had less proven reserves at the beginning of the year than at the end, even with the intervening 365 days of consumption being factored in. Odd circumstances indeed for a non-renewable and scarce resource!

The natural production theory of oil (biotic) says that crude oil results from the trapped decay products of living organisms which die and then get trapped under the Earth. This percolates at elevated temperature and pressure for millions of years. This theory is so well accepted that the American Oil Industry does not even fund the research into alternative theories, even though this one goes back to the 19th century and is predicated on some pretty weak science. This always struck me as a bizarre and unlikely series of events, that dead animals, vegetation, deserts, fields and forests would get plowed under the earth and after millions of years become oil.

Upon closer inspection the biotic theory of oil stands upon a single fact originally proposed in the 19th century. Naturally occurring petroleum is chiral, that is left-handed or right-handed. Living organisms selectively prefer one form of a hydrocarbon molecule over another whose difference is solely determined by spatial arrangements of the constituent atoms. Chemical properties, like the energy content available for combustion, are the same regardless of chirality, so as a fuel for human kind the difference is zero. It is a well known fact that synthetic chemical processes produce a racemic mixture (50/50)

> **FAST FACT**
>
> According to the Department of Energy, one barrel of crude oil, when refined, produces about 20 gallons of finished motor gasoline, 7 gallons of diesel, and 44 gallons of petroleum that make other products, such as ink, crayons, bubble gum, dish washing liquids, deodorant, eyeglasses, records, tires, ammonia, and heart valves.

of left-handed and right-handed molecules. The conclusion is that any petroleum mixture that is not a racemic distribution must have come from natural processes, i.e. the proposed biotic theory. It is another well known fact that enzymes, the molecules that make living things alive always prefer one chiral version over another, so the metabolic by-products of enzymatic metabolism always favor one over the other. This is the single fact that the biotic theory is based upon.

Circumstantial evidence is often provided to support this conjecture. Peat Bogs, tar pits, coal, and crude oil are found with this metabolic split. A petroleum chemist will tell you that organic decay gives rise to coal which in turn gives rise to crude oil that ultimately produces methane (natural gas). Methane being the end stage of this evolutionary process that occurs underground over millions and millions of years.

Petroleum prospecting involves looking for impermeable rock structures that trap moving petroleum and prevent the eventual dissipation. The rock caps form reservoirs where the petroleum sits for millions of years awaiting the drill. There are other mechanisms that could be producing the same results but with very different mechanisms producing the results. The petroleum industry in the United States has disregarded this for years, whereas the Russians have not. In 2008 Russia became the world's largest petroleum exporting country taking that title from Saudi Arabia. What might this mechanism be?

What about a larger scale source phenomena like Solar System formation? It is well known that there are copious amounts of methane in our Solar System. The gas giant planets of Jupiter and Saturn are proof of this. Methane is the most reduced form of a hydrocarbon possible and thus yields the highest energy content under oxidation (burning). It is also a chiral having neither left-handed nor right-handed orientations. Under the conventional (biotic) theory oil forms as vegetable material becomes coal, which becomes petroleum, and finally natural gas (methane) as oxygen is removed and the molecules become more and more reduced.

According to Thomas Gold, the biotic theory is wrong and he has some impressive figures with which to back up his ideas. Gold believes that naturally occurring petroleum is produced by primitive organisms trapped in the earth's permeable rock mantle. The bacteria known as methanotrophs consume methane for energy and produce the longer chain hydrocarbons as metabolic waste products. Since they are alive

World Oil Proven Reserves

At the end of each year, the world has always had more barrels of oil in its proven reserves than it started with.

Oil Proven Reserves Trends (In Billion Barrels)

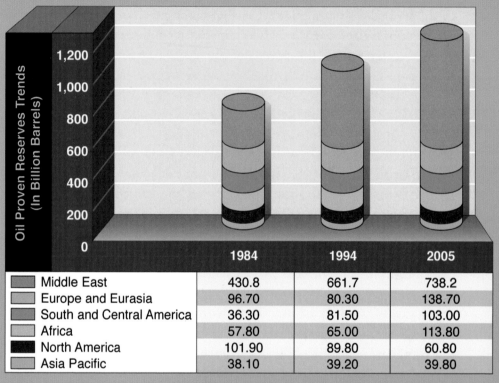

	1984	1994	2005
Middle East	430.8	661.7	738.2
Europe and Eurasia	96.70	80.30	138.70
South and Central America	36.30	81.50	103.00
Africa	57.80	65.00	113.80
North America	101.90	89.80	60.80
Asia Pacific	38.10	39.20	39.80

Note: If Candian tar sands are included, the North American total rises to 236 billion (18%).

Oil Proven Reserves 2005 (In Billion Barrels)

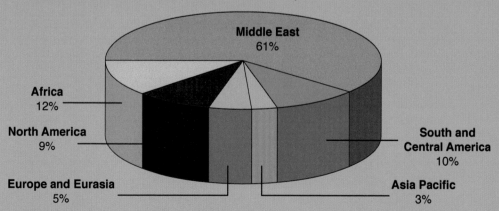

Middle East 61%

Africa 12%

North America 9%

Europe and Eurasia 5%

South and Central America 10%

Asia Pacific 3%

Taken from: British Petroleum Statistical Review, 2006.

and use enzymatic action the hydrocarbons produced will show a chiral orientation which is the same as the biotic theory. Methanotrophs are found in many places around the world in porous rocks.

To test Gold's theory a $25 million dollar drilling experiment was run in Sweden by drilling six miles into the earth. Methanotrophs and hydrocarbon residue were found in the material extracted from the bore hole. This area of Sweden is known for its dense granitic rock and lack of oil reserves. This is evidence that the abiotic theory has merit. Methane from the bowels of the earth migrates through rock pores eventually coming into contact with the methanotroph refining operations. These organisms, in their quest for life under harsh conditions, produce the black gold that powers modern society.

There is also the helium problem to contend with in the biotic theory of oil. Helium gas is found in naturally occuring petroleum reserves. Helium is the second most abundant atom in the universe. It is only formed two ways—in the initial big bang and the subsequent cooldown and in the interior of stars as part of the fusion process. Nothing on earth can manufacture it (we will ignore trace amounts resulting from thermonuclear processes since they are insignificant and just a special case of fusion). Helium wells up from the interior of the earth for whatever reason: primordial concentrations from the planet-forming, radioactive decay. Most of the helium in the world comes from wells in Texas. Helium indirectly supports the Gold model of the deep hot biosphere theory of petroleum creation. Considering the possibility that this theory is correct we can make simple estimates of what the reserves might be. If the outer 100 miles of the earth's crust are biologically active as Gold suggests and the activity is uniformly distributed then there is a lot of potential oil to be found. If oil is just .001% of the volume of the outer 100 miles of crust, then we would have an additional 5,077,713,481,834,820 barrels of oil, or about 4000 times as much as the current proved reserves. If the oil zone goes deeper then there is even more! If the oil is being replenished from below via primordial reserves left over from solar system formation then a steady state might be expected in which extraction and replenishment would balance for a long time to come. Perhaps this explains why we never seem to run out and some large oil fields continue to produce regardless of extraction rates. Some oil pools actually seem to be filling from below, which supports the deep hot biosphere theory of Thomas Gold.

The first set of calculations were originally made in 2006. What is the state of proven reserves today (2008)? Radford University offers up a nice comparison of "proven resources and recoverable resources." The high is 2272.5 billion barrels with a low of 981.4. This gives us a median of 1060, an average of 1343, a variance of 386, and standard deviation of 621. Not exactly accurate data, but these are government statistics and may be prone to some inaccuracy. This can be interpreted as this data is either proving or disproving this assertion depending on whether we like the mean, high end or the low end. A variance of 25% of the average might be considered unsure. The Department of Energy has web data on oil reserves. One of them states that total world oil reserves at the end of 2007 were 1.317 trillion barrels of oil. I am a clear winner on this one, assuming we accept the statistics as factual. Canada is a major producer of oil. Trendlines Research has a nice, albeit hodge-podge, compendium of statistics that can be found on their website. This site represents that Saudi Reserves could be as high as 900 billion barrels of oil which is more than half the currently accepted world-wide reserve figure of 1.2–1.3 trillion barrels of oil. The graphics provide information representing the difference between proven, probable and contingent resources, which hint at the fact that market forces will determine capacity as a function of price and recovery techniques.

The Oil Crisis is a Chicken Little (the sky is falling, i.e. wells are drying up) web site that advocates solar energy as a savior for civilization. This clearly demonstrates that they have no understanding of the concept of energy density. Energy density shows that fossil and nuclear (fission/fusion) are the only feasible techniques given current technology. Nature depends completely on fusion from gravitational collapse for thermodynamic energy input on a planetary scale throughout the known Universe which is a very broad statistical sample. Solar is nice for heating your pool, and good for plants with several hundred million years of technology development via evolution, but will not cut it for our technological society. Modern civilization requires the higher-density deposits from planetary collapse (an abiogenic oil source interior to the planet seeping into rock caps that we drill holes through and suck out).

This site asserts that the concept of proven oil reserves is meaningless, given that many of these statistics are from governmental agencies and are prone to institutional bias, that is, prevarication. This is not an unreasonable concept.

Some people claim that oil fields are replenishing themselves, thereby reducing the chance of running dry.

The critical reader might comment that only using web resources which run the gamut of credibility from high, to questionable, to silly and as such is specious. This is a point well taken, but most reliable sources of information now post to the Internet, and the Internet has hundreds of millions to billions of "fact checkers" that the diligent reader can quickly consult for guidance.

The proven reserves concept may be meaningless as it is so tenuous as to be devoid of meaning. The statistics of proven oil reserves are largely from government agencies, petroleum industry concerns, and cranks like oildrum, peakoil, and hubbert. It is my opinion that history has demonstrated they are wrong, that proven reserves go up over time, and currency-adjusted prices go down.

The twentieth century saw unprecedented advances in man's understanding of the physical processes that govern the Universe. None of these discoveries are used in the biotic theory. It just gets propounded over and over by the experts. No funding is available for alternative theories. Yet history has shown that science is mostly arrogant when it is "certain," which typically is just before the next big breakthrough. Galileo overthrew the earth-centric universe. Maxwell triumphed over Faraday, Einstein triumphed over the continuum hypothesis, quantum mechanics triumphed over classical mechanics. Quantum field theory, when united with special relativity, triumphed over quantum mechanics. Evolution over creationism. General relativity over Special relativity. Now we have the dark matter problem. A pattern is being expounded upon. History shows that the expert consensus of the tenured does not control what comes next, it only clings to its position as long as it can.

However, the sad commentary is that our society is becoming reactionary: dramatic adjustments occur through crisis which lead to poorly planned and executed government programs (Iraq and Katrina come to mind). Oil producers have little incentive to admit that their product is a low profit margin commodity item whose supply is increasing thus forcing prices down when they have been showered with incentives, tax credits and outright gifts.

In closing I offer up two facts: first that oil is denominated in dollars worldwide, and second that the dollar has lost more than half of its value against gold during the Bush II Presidency. Since gold is relatively constant in supply this extrapolates that oil is actually getting cheaper. During the past eight years the price has basically doubled to the American consumer, yet purchasing power has decreased at a greater rate thanks to the Federal Reserve Bank inflation via M1 money supply increases.

It currently looks like the assertion that oil supply is increasing and not decreasing is more credible than Dr. Hubbert's peak oil. My facts are unchecked and statistically insignificant which puts me on an equal footing with government agencies and cranks. So let your wallet do the talking at the pump and rely on the dispassionate market to iterate through supply and demand via the price mechanism (billions of daily fact checkers here). It sure works better than the Synfuels Corporation!

Why then would the oil industry cry shortage in such a period of abundance? There is nothing like a perceived crisis to suspend rational thought and behavior. This happened during the seventies when stagflation ruled the day and we were running out of oil (again), in spite of the proven reserve facts. Current "expert" consumption rates indicate the pool will run dry this century, but if history is any guide at the end of this century there will be more proven reserves than at the beginning of the century (which was the case with the last one). If Freeman Dyson thinks Thomas Gold is on to something, as a Nobel Laureate co-inventor of Quantum Electrodynamics (QED) he carries a fair amount of intellectual weight.

The basic thesis here is that lots of eco-nuts, and policy wonks think that oil production has peaked and that doom is around the proverbial corner (as it always seems to be, no matter how many corners we safely round). Even if it were true, and these reserves were rapidly dwindling (the data shows they are not) the free market will adjust and other forms of energy will become available. Nothing rations supply accurately like price, that is, market forces, and historically these are just the things not allowed to function, instead we get myriads of laws, regulations, incentives, and taxpayer funded boondoggles (Synfuel Corporation comes to mind) perverting the process.

If this thesis is correct then this is another non-issue. At the end of this year, like the end of every year in the past we will have more proven reserves than we did at the beginning. Odd considering we are discussing what is purported to be an increasingly scarce resource, but the politicians and their funding dependent sycophants never let the truth interfere with a good story.

EVALUATING THE AUTHOR'S ARGUMENTS:

In the viewpoint you just read, the author bases his argument on Thomas Gold's hot biosphere theory of oil production. Who is Thomas Gold? What do you think of his theory? Does he have credentials to back up his oil theory? Which theory makes more sense to you?

Chapter 2

What Problems Come from Using Oil as an Energy Source?

Pollution and smog are among the most common problems associated with using oil to produce energy.

Viewpoint

1

U.S. Dependency on Oil Constitutes a Security Threat

Gal Luft

"America's oil policy is unsustainable and . . . subjects the nation to grave risks."

In the following viewpoint Gal Luft argues that America's dependency on oil from the Persian Gulf makes it vulnerable to terrorism, war, and political instability. America relies on foreign oil for 60 percent of its oil resources, he explains, which leaves it at the mercy of foreign distributors. Worse, says Luft, the money the United States spends on foreign oil often ends up in the hands of terrorist organizations and despotic regimes, the very groups who threaten U.S. security. For these reasons, Luft urges the United States to break its dependency on foreign oil in order to protect itself against actors who may use America's need for oil or its valuable petrodollars to nefarious ends.

Gal Luft is executive director of the Institute for the Analysis of Global Security (IAGS) and the cochair of the Set America Free Coalition. He specializes in strategy, geopolitics, terrorism, the Middle East, and energy security.

Gal Luft, "America's Oil Dependence and Its Implications for U.S. Middle East Policy," in testimony before the Senate Foreign Relations Subcommittee on Near Eastern and South Asian Affairs, October 20, 2005.

AS YOU READ, CONSIDER THE FOLLOWING QUESTIONS:
1. According to the author, how many millions of barrels of oil currently come from the Middle East? How many are expected to come from the Middle East in the future?
2. Who are jihadists and how do petrodollars end up in their hands, according to Luft?
3. What three oil-exporting countries did the Bush administration waive sanctions against for human trafficking, according to the author?

As consumer of a quarter of the world's oil supply and holder of a mere three percent of global oil reserves the U.S. is heavily dependent on foreign oil and a growing share of this oil comes from the Persian Gulf. America's dependence on foreign oil has increased from 30 percent in 1973, when OPEC [Organization of Petroleum Exporting Countries] imposed its oil embargo, to 60 percent today [October 2005]. According to the Department of Energy this dependence is projected to reach 70 percent by 2025. In the wake of the war on terrorism, the rise of China and India and growing voices within the oil industry that "the era of easy oil is over" it has become apparent to many that America's oil policy is unsustainable and that such a policy subjects the nation to grave risks.

Oil Dictates U.S. Foreign Policy

Since the 1945 meeting between President Franklin Roosevelt and King Abdul Aziz ibn Saud, the founder of the Saudi monarchy, U.S. foreign policy has been subservient to the nation's energy needs. Access to the Persian Gulf oil required robust and costly military presence in the region and frequent interventions. Worse, the U.S. has been forced to coddle some of the world's worst despots just because they held the key to our prosperity hence compromising American values and principles.

Of the 11 million barrels per day (mbd) the U.S. imports today [October 2005] close to 3mbd come from the Middle East. But in the years to come dependence on the Middle East is projected to increase by leaps and bounds. The reason is that reserves outside of the Middle East are being depleted at a much faster rate than those in the region. The overall reserves-to-production ratio—an indicator of how long proven reserves would last at current production rates—outside of the Middle East is about 15 years comparing to roughly 80 years in the Middle East. According to Exxon Corporation and PFC Energy, non-OPEC production, including Russia and West Africa will peak within a decade. At that point the amount of oil found outside of the Middle East will decline steeply, putting OPEC in the driver seat of the world economy.

These projections require that we take a sober long term look at the impact of our growing dependence on our strategic posture in the Middle East.

Increased Oil Revenues Support Terrorists

Oil prices are not going down any time soon. The rise in oil prices will yield large financial surpluses to the Middle Eastern oil producers. This

Insurgents in Iraq have made a point of attacking sites involved in Iraq's oil industry, making some people worry about the potential for the United States to be hurt by our reliance on oil imported from the Middle East.

petrodollar windfall will strengthen the jihadists while undermining the strategic relationship the region's oil producers have with the U.S.

As President [George W.] Bush said last April [2005], U.S. dependence on overseas oil is a "foreign tax on the American people." Indeed, oil imports constitute a quarter of the U.S. trade deficit and are a major contributor to the loss of jobs and investment opportunities. According to a study on the hidden cost of oil by the National Defense Council Foundation, the periodic oil shocks the U.S. has experienced since the 1973 Arab oil embargo cost the economy almost $2.5 trillion. More importantly, while the U.S. economy is bleeding, oil-producing nations increase their oil revenues dramatically to the detriment of our national security. The numbers speak for themselves: In November 2001, a barrel of oil was selling for

> **FAST FACT**
>
> The United States receives much of its imported oil from unstable and sometimes unfriendly nations, including Saudi Arabia, Nigeria, Algeria, Iraq, Colombia, and Libya.

$18. In less than four years the price jumped to $70. This means that Saudi Arabia, which exports about 10 mbd, receives an extra half billion dollars every day from consuming nations and Iran, which exports 2.5 mbd, an extra $125 million. This windfall benefits the non-democratic governments of the Middle East and other producers and finds its way to the jihadists committed to America's destruction as petrodollars trickle their way through charities and government handouts to madrassas and mosques, as well as outright support of terrorist groups.

It is widely accepted that Saudi Arabia's oil wealth has directly enabled the spread of Wahhabism [a conservative sect of Islam] around the world. The Saudis use oil funds to control most of the Arabic language media and are now moving to gain growing control over Western media. Only last month [September 2005] Saudi Prince Al-Waleed bin Talal, the world's fifth richest man, purchased 5.46 percent of Fox News corporation.

Funding Both Sides in the War on Terrorism

Petrodollars garnered from the U.S. and other countries are also being used by Saudi Arabia systematically to provide social services, build "Islamic centers" and schools, pay preachers' salaries and, in some cases,

Where Are the World's Oil Reserves?

Most of the world's oil is in the Middle East, but each region has a little.

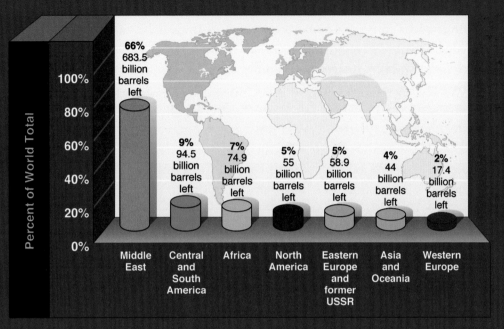

Taken from: Public Broadcasting Service, 2007.

fund terror organizations. In July 2005 undersecretary of the Treasury Stuart Levey testifying before the Senate Committee on Banking, Housing, and Urban Affairs noted "Wealthy Saudi financiers and charities have funded terrorist organizations and causes that support terrorism and the ideology that fuels the terrorists' agenda. Even today [October 2005], we believe that Saudi donors may still be a significant source of terrorist financing, including for the insurgency in Iraq."

The U.S. is in an odd situation in which it is funding both sides in the war on terrorism. We finance the defense of the Free World against its sworn enemies through our tax dollars. And at the same time we support hostile regimes through the transfer of petrodollars. If we don't change course we will bleed more dollars each year as our enemies gather strength. Steady increase in world demand for oil means further enrichment of the corrupt and dictatorial regimes in the Persian Gulf and continued access of terrorist groups to a viable financial network which allows them to remain a lethal threat to the U.S. and its allies. . . .

An Inconsistent Oil Policy

America's current oil policy is inconsistent with the hallmark of the Bush Administration's foreign policy: bringing democracy and political reform to areas where democracy is in deficit. Oil revenues help despots sustain anti democratic social and political systems giving them disincentives to embrace social and economic reforms. Our dependence on foreign oil often prevents the U.S. from expressing its true feelings about some of the conducts and practices of oil producing countries. Only last month [September 2005] the Bush Administration waived sanctions against Saudi Arabia, Kuwait and Ecuador, three of the world's worst offenders in human trafficking. In the case of Saudi Arabia and Kuwait the administration's explanation was that it was "in U.S. interest to continue democracy programs and security cooperation in the war on terrorism." One could only wonder if those two countries would have received the same treatment had they been major exporters of watermelons. . . .

Four years after September 11 it is essential that we view our geopolitical situation in the context of our oil dependence and realize that it will be extremely difficult to win the war on terror and spread democracy around the world as long as we continue to send petrodollars to those who do not share our vision and values. As long as the U.S. remains dependent on oil to the degree that its does today, its dependence on the Middle East will grow. The U.S. can no longer afford to postpone urgent action to strengthen its energy security and it must begin a bold process toward reducing its demand for oil.

EVALUATING THE AUTHOR'S ARGUMENTS:

In the viewpoint you just read, Gal Luft states that the United States is "funding both sides in the war on terrorism." Clarify what he means by this statement. Do you think he is right? Explain your answer thoroughly.

Viewpoint 2

U.S. Dependency on Oil Does Not Constitute a Security Threat

Philip E. Auerswald

"Oil can't easily be used as a strategic instrument of aggression against the United States."

In the following viewpoint author Philip E. Auerswald argues that America's reliance on foreign oil does not make it vulnerable to terrorism, war, or political or economic instability. He argues that oil is too valuable to be used as a strategic aggressive weapon. Foreign oil producers such as Saudi Arabia need oil profits more than the United States needs oil and would be unwilling to risk a disruption in revenue in order to attack or interrupt supply to the United States. Because of this, the security threat to America from these oil-producing nations is often exaggerated and minimal, concludes Auerswald.

Auerswald is the director of the Center for Science and Technology Policy at George Mason University's School of Public Policy. He has been a consultant to the National Academies of Science, the Commonwealth of Massachusetts, and the National Institute of Standards and Technology.

Philip E. Auerswald, "Let's Call an End to Oil Alarmism," *International Herald Tribune,* January 23, 2007. Reprinted with permission of Pars International.

O il prices have ended their steep ascent—for now—and are headed downward. The near-universal alarm among politicians, pundits and consumers over America's dependency on foreign oil has yielded to a wary sense of relief. But both the prior alarm and the current relief are misguided.

Dependence on Foreign Oil Is Not a Security Threat

Few propositions are at once more widely accepted and less rooted in fact than the notion tha t increasing U.S. reliance on foreign oil is a security threat requiring urgent action. Such concern reflects a view of markets that has been rendered obsolete by globalization. The oft-stated objective of "energy independence" is as devoid of substance and irrelevant to our security as "computer independence" or "clothing independence."

Consider the following facts:

Oil producers don't like oil prices that are "too high." Adel al-Jubeir, foreign policy adviser to Crown Prince Abdullah of Saudi Arabia, offered this frank assessment to *The Wall Street Journal* in 2004, just as oil prices began to increase sharply: "We've got almost 30 percent of the world's oil. For us, the objective is to assure that oil remains an economically competitive source of energy. Oil prices that are too high

> **FAST FACT**
>
> Canada is consistently among the top suppliers of oil to the United States, along with Mexico, the Virgin Islands, Kuwait, the United Kingdom, and Norway, all of whom maintain good relations with America.

reduce demand growth for oil and encourage the development of alternative energy sources."

In response, Saudi Arabia ramped up oil production, from 8.5 million barrels per day in 2002 to 11.1 million in 2005. Far more dependent on oil revenue than the West is on oil, the Saudis lose if a high price today prompts their customers to develop substitutes.

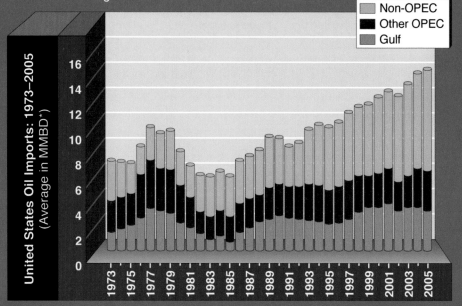

America's Oil Imports Do Not Threaten Its Security

America's top three petroleum suppliers are Canada, Mexico, and Venezuela, all of which have good relations with the United States.

Legend:
- Non-OPEC
- Other OPEC
- Gulf

United States Oil Imports: 1973–2005 (Average in MMBD*) — Y-axis: 0, 2, 4, 6, 8, 10, 12, 14, 16 — X-axis years: 1973, 1975, 1977, 1979, 1981, 1983, 1985, 1987, 1989, 1991, 1993, 1995, 1997, 1999, 2001, 2003, 2005

U.S. Petroleum Imports: Top 15 Countries
(Average in MMBD)

Country	Imports in 2005	Country	Imports in 2005
Canada	2.172	Ecuador	0.282
Mexico	1.646	Virgin Islands	0.326
Venezuela	1.506	Kuwait	0.231
Saudi Arabia	1.523	Russia	0.398
Nigeria	1.147	Brazil	0.156
Angola	0.465	UK	0.387
Algeria	0.477	Norway	0.230
Iraq	0.522		

* millions of barrels per day

Taken from: EIA.

Oil Is Too Valuable to Be Used as a Weapon

The upswing in the price of many commodities, including oil, over the past five years reflects positive economic developments. In the next two decades or so, most of the world's population—including a couple of billion in China and India—will finally become full partners in the world economy.

This is good news. For the foreseeable future potential supply problems—whether caused by terrorism, political disputes or other issues in the Middle East or elsewhere—will have far less of an impact on prices than these changes on the demand side.

Oil can't easily be used as a strategic instrument of aggression against the United States. Petro-alarmism focused on the Middle East often emphasizes the concentration of oil reserves and spare production capacity in a few oil-producing nations, particularly Saudi Arabia. But reserves are only useful as a strategic weapon in pushing prices down. Only by withholding output—and threatening their own livelihood—can producers push prices higher.

Higher Fuel Prices Have Minimal Impact

The impact of higher fuel prices on most U.S. consumers is minimal. From 1980 to 2005, the share of consumer spending on energy dropped from 8 percent to 6 percent; the 2006 figure will be higher, but not enough to signal a consumer calamity. True, the impacts of higher energy prices are unevenly felt. But the fact that U.S. oil companies celebrate record profits while the rural poor economize on trips to the grocery store is a matter of domestic politics, not international security.

Oil price movements do not have a major impact on the economy as a whole. What actual damage did the recent oil price run-up cause? When the price of oil doubled, as many long dreaded, which crippling effects were observed? None. Economic growth continued apace. Any slowing had more to do with higher interest rates. The U.S. economy is far more adaptable than petro-alarmists would have us believe.

Imported Oil Does Not Make Us Vulnerable

Regardless of the cause, rising oil prices during this decade have helped the national interest in the long term. In an open society with a market

It has been suggested that Arabs would also be hurt by attempts to stop the flow of oil to the United States since people in the Middle East earn their living supporting the oil industry.

economy, only high prices have the brute power to compel the adjustments required to address the real energy-related challenge facing us: global climate change. For this reason, the public should worry not that oil prices might climb again, but rather that they might continue to fall. Energy independence is a hollow objective, but addressing threats from climate change is not.

The notion that oil imports lead to energy insecurity suits environmentalists, military hawks, foreign-policy idealists, subsidy-seeking oil executives and even anti-U.S. propagandists, but it does not fit the facts. Politicians and pundits alike would do well to put this treasured, but frayed, idea aside.

EVALUATING THE AUTHORS' ARGUMENTS:

Philip E. Auerswald argues that America's dependence on foreign oil does not constitute a security threat. How do you think Gal Luft, author of the previous viewpoint, would respond to this claim? Support your answer with evidence from the text.

Oil Drilling Will Ruin Wildlife Refuges

U.S. PIRG Education Fund

"It just does not make sense to ruin one of America's last wild places for a few months' worth of oil."

In the following viewpoint the U.S. PIRG Education Fund argues that drilling for oil and gas in the Arctic National Wildlife Refuge (ANWR) will ruin one of America's last wild places. The authors argue that, contrary to Bush administration claims, drilling in the refuge will not reduce America's dependence on foreign oil because ANWR only contains a few months' worth of oil that would not be available for years to come. This small amount of oil is especially not worth it when one realizes that drilling in ANWR would ruin the wildlife and habitat of one of the last wild places in the world. The authors argue ANWR would become vulnerable to toxic spills, pollution, and unlimited development that would irrevocably change the Arctic ecosystem. To prevent this, the authors urge the United States to protect the Arctic National Wildlife Refuge from oil drilling.

"Saving America's Arctic: Dispelling Myths About Drilling in the Arctic National Wildlife Refuge," *www.uspirg.org,* September 2005. Reproduced by permission.

The U.S. PIRG Education Fund is the research and policy center for U.S. PIRG, the national association of the state Public Interest Research Groups.

AS YOU READ, CONSIDER THE FOLLOWING QUESTIONS:
  1. What makes the Arctic National Wildlife Refuge a wild, natural wonder, according to the authors?
  2. How many oil spills did Alaska's North Slope experience between 1996 and 2004, according to the authors?
  3. What percent of the world's oil could ANWR produce, according to the authors?

The coastal plain of the Arctic National Wildlife Refuge [ANWR] is truly one of America's last wild places. It contains no roads, trails, or structures, so you must fly, boat, or walk to get there. It is a pristine habitat, one that supports large populations of migratory birds, caribou, muskoxen, all three species of bear, wolves, Dall sheep, and snow geese. The annual migration of the 129,000-member caribou herd evokes images of the long-gone buffalo herds of the Great Plains.

The coastal plain of the Arctic Refuge is the only area along Alaska's entire North Slope that is not currently open for oil and gas exploration. Unfortunately, oil companies such as ExxonMobil and their allies in the Bush administration and Congress are pushing to drill in the coastal plain of the Arctic Refuge, endangering one of America's last wild places for a few months' worth of oil and gas.

Drilling advocates have made several different arguments to try to garner more support for drilling in the Arctic National Wildlife Refuge. These arguments simply do not stand up to the facts. . . .

A Natural Wonder
In 1960, President Dwight Eisenhower established the Arctic National Wildlife Range in recognition of the area's unparalleled scenic, wildlife and recreational values. In 1980, Congress renamed the Range as the Arctic National Wildlife Refuge and enlarged the Refuge to 19 million

acres. Most of the former Range became a part of the Wilderness Preservation System. The only area not designated as wilderness was the 1.5 million acre coastal plain. Known as Section 1002, the coastal plain was designated as a study area at the behest of the oil and gas industry. As a study area, the coastal plain is not open to drilling, nor is it permanently protected from drilling or development.

The coastal plain is the only area along Alaska's entire North Slope that is not open to oil and gas exploration. It is also one of the most pristine. There are no roads, developments, or trails. The Refuge is the lone conservation area in the nation that provides a complete range of Arctic and subarctic ecosystems and the only wholly unspoiled part of America's Arctic. As one of the last true vestiges of a world untouched by humans and a natural wonder to pass on to the next generation, it deserves the highest level of protection. . . .

ANWR Does Not Contain Much Oil

Drilling in the Arctic Refuge will not lower prices at the pump. Allowing oil drilling in the coastal plain of the Arctic Refuge will not lower the price of a gallon of gasoline. First, the Arctic Refuge does not hold enough oil to affect the world market. Second, OPEC producers and other oil-producing nations could reduce output to counter any increase in U.S. output to keep oil prices high.

The Arctic Refuge would yield too little oil to influence prices. The U.S. Geological Survey has concluded that the Arctic Refuge contains less oil than the U.S. consumes in a year. Moreover, the amount of oil likely to be recovered from the Arctic Refuge would be no more than one-third of one percent (0.3%) of the world's oil reserves. The Bush administration's own Energy Information Administration (EIA) found that drilling in the Arctic Refuge would do nothing to lower gasoline prices at the pump in the short term and almost nothing over the long term, as drilling would

Some fear that expanding oil drilling in Alaska could jeopardize wildlife like the musk ox that are native to the region.

reduce gasoline prices by less than a penny-and-a-half a gallon and not until 2025. . . .

Drilling in the Arctic Refuge will not reduce America's dependence on foreign oil. According to EIA, oil from the Arctic Refuge would only reduce oil imports by about two to four percent in 2025. At its peak, the Arctic Refuge likely would provide only 7/10 of one percent (0.7%) of projected world oil production and would decline thereafter.

Oil Drilling Hurts the Environment

Toxic spills and air pollution from year-round oil and gas drilling are polluting Alaska's fragile North Slope, home to Prudhoe Bay and 26 other producing fields that sprawl across 1,000 square miles, an area the size of Rhode Island. This industrial complex includes more than 4,800 exploratory and production wells, 223 production and exploratory drill pads, more than 500 miles of roads, 1,800 miles of trunk and feeder pipes in more than 600 miles of pipeline corridors, two refineries, 20 airports, 107 gravel pads for living quarters and other support facilities, five docks and gravel causeways, 36 gravel mines, and a total of 28 production plants, gas processing facilities, seawater treatment plants, and power plants. Prudhoe Bay air pollution emissions have been detected nearly 200 miles away in Barrow, Alaska.

Oil Spills Are Increasing

Oil spills on the North Slope are on the rise. According to data reported to the Alaska Department of Environmental Conservation, Alaska's North Slope experienced 4,532 spills between 1996 and 2004, an average of 504 spills annually. Overall, reported spills in this area increased by 33 percent between 1996 and 2004, reaching a high of 678 spills in 2002. These spills released a total of 1.9 million gallons of crude oil, diesel, drilling fluids and waste, and other substances into the delicate Arctic environment. In 2004 alone, 554 spills were reported on the North Slope, or one spill every 16 hours.

Some of the recent oil spills have been significant. For example:

- On April 12, 2005, a high-pressure oil line sprang a leak at BP's Drill Site 14 in Prudhoe Bay. About 1.4 million cubic feet of natural gas and an unknown amount of crude oil were sprayed over an area measuring nearly a mile in length and 300 feet in width.
- On March 26, 2005, a buried pipe broke for unknown reasons, spilling about 111,300 gallons of water over two acres of frozen tundra at a ConocoPhillips gravel production site in Kuparuk, the North Slope's biggest oil field after Prudhoe Bay. The spilled water contained about 50 gallons of crude oil; but much of the water was seawater, and the salt can kill tundra plant life just as crude oil can. About 80 workers toiled around the clock for three weeks to clean up the spill, which ranked as one of the largest industrial spills ever in the North Slope oil fields. . . .

A Disruption of Wildlife

This industrialization has more than cosmetic consequences. Seismic exploration activities disturb wildlife. Polar bears have been known to abandon their dens after seismic exploration trucks drove nearby. Damage to underlying tundra, which serves as food and shelter to many Arctic animals, also can last for decades. Decreased caribou calving within a four kilometer zone of pipelines and roads shows that the "extent of avoidance greatly exceeds the physical 'footprint' of an oil-field complex," according to caribou biologists.

Finally, there is no requirement that the 2,000 acres of production and support facilities be in one contiguous area. As with the oil fields to the west of the Arctic Refuge, development could and would be spread out over a large area. Indeed, according to the United States Geological Survey, oil under the coastal plain is not concentrated in one large reservoir but is spread under the coastal plain in numerous small deposits. To produce oil from this vast area, therefore, supporting infrastructure would stretch across the coastal plain; we likely would see a sprawling spider web of development. No matter how well done, oil exploration and development will industrialize a unique, wild area that is the biological heart of the Refuge.

A Wildlife Haven

Drilling for oil in this pristine haven for wildlife would disrupt and ultimately destroy one of America's last remaining truly wild places. Instead of pushing to drill in the Arctic Refuge, the Bush administration should act to make our cars and SUVs go farther on a gallon of gasoline. . . .

What Problems Come from Using Oil as an Energy Source?   75

A century ago, a short-sighted development policy almost wiped out the buffalo of the Great Plains. The buffalo narrowly survived, but the magnificent prairie is gone. One hundred years later, the Arctic Refuge is facing the same kind of threat. We must not let that happen to the Arctic Refuge and the wildlife it supports. It just does not make sense to ruin one of America's last wild places for a few months' worth of oil.

EVALUATING THE AUTHORS' ARGUMENTS:

In the viewpoint you just read, the authors use history, facts, and examples to make their argument that ANWR should not be opened for drilling. They do not, however, use any quotations to support their points. If you were to rewrite this viewpoint and insert quotations, what authorities, voices, or sources might you quote from? Where would you place these quotations to bolster the points made by the authors?

Oil Drilling Will Not Ruin Wildlife Refuges

Frank Murkowski

"The facts demonstrate that ANWR . . .can be developed without significantly impacting the North Slope environment."

In the following viewpoint Frank Murkowski argues that drilling for oil will not harm wildlife refuges, specifically the Arctic National Wildlife Refuge (ANWR) located in Alaska. Murkowski argues that the United States' need for energy warrants the exploration of domestic energy sources; this is the only way to reduce America's reliance on foreign oil. The author claims that oil reserves in ANWR could supply the United States with oil for the next twenty-five years. Murkowski further claims that it is possible to develop these oil fields in an environmentally responsible way that will not harm wildlife and the surrounding habitat. He concludes that ANWR should be opened to drilling because the United States can reap much-needed conflict-free oil at little risk to the environment.

Frank Murkowski was the governor of Alaska from 2002–2006. He also served as the chairman of the National Governors Association Natural Resources Committee.

"Testimony by Governor Frank Murkowski on Behalf of The National Governors Association: Before the Committee on Energy and Commerce," U.S. House of Representatives, February 10, 2005. Reproduced by permission of Frank Murkowski.

I appreciate the opportunity to provide comments to this committee as you consider legislation to create a comprehensive energy policy for the United States. The National Governors Association supports an energy policy that balances energy production, efficiency and conservation, environmental quality, and a healthy economy. Our policy maintains that energy issues must be addressed nationally, while still recognizing state and local authority over environmental and land use issues.

Oil Development Is Necessary—Especially in Alaska

We believe that the solution to the need for energy will require increased conservation and energy efficiency as well as exploration of new energy supplies. That exploration should include environmentally responsible development of traditional fossil fuel sources and greater reliance on alternative and renewable sources.

FAST FACT

Proponents of drilling in ANWR say that less than two thousand acres of land would be affected by Arctic drilling—about the size of a South Carolina farm.

In particular, we think the titles of the Conference agreement dealing with energy efficiency and renewable energy are very positive and will provide incentives for programs that help encourage new techniques and technologies. We support provisions of the oil and gas title that will promote new domestic production through exploration and development of additional petroleum reserves and encourage effective market-based measures that will support production of natural gas supplies and development of infrastructure in an environmentally sound manner.

We also would like to see a reduction in the impediments that limit natural gas production, however, we are mindful that many states support drilling moratoria off their shores. We believe that federal land management agencies should have the resources available to participate and coordinate with states regarding federal decisions about energy

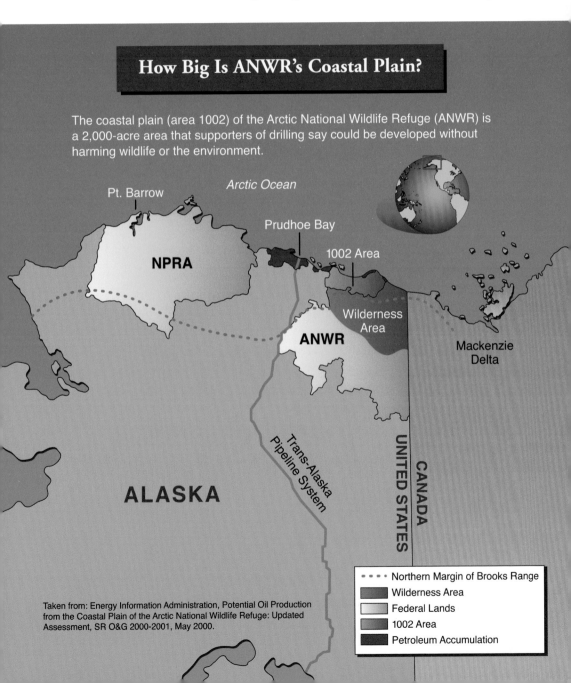

How Big Is ANWR's Coastal Plain?

The coastal plain (area 1002) of the Arctic National Wildlife Refuge (ANWR) is a 2,000-acre area that supporters of drilling say could be developed without harming wildlife or the environment.

Arctic Ocean

Pt. Barrow

Prudhoe Bay

1002 Area

NPRA

Wilderness Area

ANWR

Mackenzie Delta

Trans-Alaska Pipeline System

ALASKA

UNITED STATES

CANADA

Taken from: Energy Information Administration, Potential Oil Production from the Coastal Plain of the Arctic National Wildlife Refuge: Updated Assessment, SR O&G 2000-2001, May 2000.

- - - - Northern Margin of Brooks Range
Wilderness Area
Federal Lands
1002 Area
Petroleum Accumulation

exploration and production on federal lands. And of course, we continue our support for the Alaska natural gas pipeline. . . .

ANWR's Promising Oil Supply

The Coastal Plain of ANWR has been determined to be the most promising unexplored petroleum province in North America, the only area with the potential to discover an "elephant" field like Prudhoe Bay. Thus, the U.S. Geological Survey has estimated that the amount of technically recoverable oil beneath the Coastal Plain ranges between 5.7 billion (95% probability) and 15.9 billion barrels (5% probability) at $25 per barrel. At $50 per barrel, all of the known physical reserves would be economic, thereby increasing these estimates significantly. The Coastal Plain may also contain significant deposits of natural gas.

Oil from ANWR represents a secure domestic supply, which could help fulfill U.S. demand for twenty-five years or more. Government studies suggest that the Coastal Plain could produce a ten year sustained rate of one million barrels per day.

The Benefits of Developing ANWR

The development of ANWR would reduce U.S. dependence on unstable foreign sources of crude oil, such as oil from the Middle East and OPEC [Organization of the Petroleum Exporting Countries] coun-

Oil drilling near Deadhorse, Alaska, does not appear to have harmed the caribou population in the area.

tries. ANWR oil would reduce the U.S. trade deficit, a large percentage of which is directly attributable to the importation of crude oil, now [February 2005] totaling approximately 60% of daily consumption and rising.

Incremental production from the Coastal Plain of ANWR should help reduce price volatility in the US. In this regard, recent supply disruptions affecting Nigeria, Iraq, Norway, and the Gulf of Mexico illustrate how even relatively low levels of production can influence the world price of oil.

ANWR development would create hundreds of thousands of American jobs affecting virtually every state by providing a secure supply of petroleum and by creating a demand for goods and services.

Oil and gas development in ANWR is not a panacea. Such development should be part of an energy policy which includes the development of alternative fuels, fuel efficiency, conservation, and other measures. However, gasoline and other products refined from crude oil will continue to fuel our transportation system for the foreseeable future.

Minimal Impact on the Environment
Experience on the North Slope demonstrates that ANWR can be developed in a manner that protects the environment and which provides greater safeguards than exist in other parts of the world:

- Advanced technology such as horizontal drilling, multiple well completions, and smaller drilling pads, ensures that the footprint of development would be less than 2,000 acres (approximately the size of an average farm in South Carolina or the equivalent of one letter on the front page of the *New York Times*).
- The Coastal Plain of ANWR comprises approximately 1.5 million acres in a National Wildlife Refuge that includes over 19 million acres (the size of South Carolina) of which 8 million acres has been designated by Congress as wilderness and hence would be off limits to any commercial activity.
- Oil development is compatible with the protection of wildlife and their habitat. For example, North Slope caribou herds have remained healthy throughout previous oil development. In fact, the Central Arctic caribou herd, which is located in and around Prudhoe Bay, has increased 10 fold in the last 20 years.

• For most of the year, the Coastal Plain of ANWR is a frozen, desolate area. Experience demonstrates that seasonal restrictions and other environmental stipulations can be utilized to protect caribou calving (6 weeks in the summer), migratory birds, and fish.

Many Supporters

Recognizing the employment and economic benefits that would accrue to them, the Inupiat Eskimos of the North Slope generally support oil development in the Coastal Plain. In this regard, most residents of the village of Kaktovik, which is located on the Coastal Plain, have expressed their support for development.

For the past 5 years, the administration of President George W. Bush has strongly supported responsible oil development in the Coastal Plain of ANWR in recognition of the economic and national security benefits that would accrue to the nation. The Bush administration has estimated for budgetary purposes that the initial phase of ANWR development would generate $1.2 billion to the Federal treasury in Fiscal Year 2007.

Responsible oil and gas development in the Coastal Plain is supported by a broad spectrum of groups and organizations, including businesses, labor unions, petroleum users and others. ANWR has become a symbol in the philosophical debate over development versus protection. However, as the preceding indicates, the facts demonstrate that ANWR, with its concomitant benefits, can be developed without significantly impacting the North Slope environment.

EVALUATING THE AUTHORS' ARGUMENTS:

In this viewpoint Murkowski argues that the U.S. government can successfully develop oil fields in Alaska while also protecting habitat and wildlife. How do you think the author of the preceding viewpoint, the U.S. PIRG Education Fund, might respond to this argument? Explain your answer using evidence from the texts.

Gas-Powered Vehicles Dangerously Pollute the Environment

Douglas Houston, Jun Wu, Paul Ong, and Arthur Winer

"Subjects who live near roadways with a high volume of diesel vehicles are more likely to suffer from respiratory ailments, . . . leukemia and higher mortality rates."

In the following viewpoint Douglas Houston, Jun Wu, Paul Ong, and Arthur Winer argue that vehicles that run on gasoline are a threat to the environment and human health. They claim gas-powered vehicles produce dangerous air pollutants that cause respiratory ailments, cancer, and high mortality rates. Reducing vehicle emissions must become a national priority to protect both the environment and human health, they say. To remedy the problem, the authors suggest that diesel vehicles be equipped with advanced pollution control technology; schools, residences, playgrounds, and medical facilities be located away from roads and other pollution sources; and transportation projects be limited in the amount of toxic matter they produce.

Douglas Houston, Jun Wu, Paul Ong, and Arthur Winer, "Down to the Meter: Localized Vehicle Pollution Matters," *Access*, Fall 2006, pp. 22–27. Reproduced by permission of the authors.

Houston is a PhD candidate in urban planning at the University of California at Los Angeles. Wu is assistant professor of public health at the University of California at Irvine. Ong is professor of urban planning and Winer is professor of environmental health sciences, both at the University of California at Los Angeles.

AS YOU READ, CONSIDER THE FOLLOWING QUESTIONS:
1. Name six diseases associated with exposure to vehicle-related pollutants.
2. According to the authors, why are children particularly prone to air pollution from cars?
3. How close are 10 percent of public schools and 19 percent of state-licensed child care providers located to a major freeway, according to the authors?

Air pollution control programs have helped improve many aspects of regional air quality over the past thirty years despite tremendous growth in both population and vehicle-miles traveled. However, regional strategies to confront vehicle-related pollution are proving to be insufficient to protect the health of those who live, work, attend school, or play near major roadways. Recent air pollution and epidemiological findings suggest that harmful vehicle-related pollutants and their associated adverse health effects concentrate within a couple hundred meters of heavily traveled freeways and thoroughfares. We're just beginning to understand the health and economic costs of such localized effects, and we still know little about who is exposed to these pollutants.

Vehicle-Related Pollutants Are Highly Toxic

Recent field studies indicate that vehicle-related pollutants such as ultrafine particles, black carbon, and carbon monoxide are highly concentrated immediately downwind from major roadways. Their relative concentration declines by as much as sixty percent at 100 meters downwind, drops to near background levels at about 200 meters, and are indistinguishable from background ambient concentrations at 300 meters. Among vehicle-related pollutants, ultra-fine particles are especially worrisome since they are capable of penetrating cell walls and the blood-brain barrier and can be easily absorbed into vital organs. Diesel exhaust particulate is also a great concern as evidence is rapidly accumulating that subjects who live near roadways with a high volume of diesel vehicles are more likely to suffer from respiratory ailments, childhood cancer, brain cancer, leukemia and higher mortality rates than people who live more than 300 meters away from such roadways. Vehicle-related air pollutants have also been associated with respiratory illness, impaired

Cheryl Baldenweg of the Center for Biological Defense wears a surgical mask and holds up a diagram showing high readings of ground-level ozone in Los Angeles.

lung function, and increased infant mortality. A Los Angeles County study found that pregnant women who reside within 750 feet of heavily traveled roads face a ten to twenty percent higher risk of early birth and low-birth-weight babies.

Exposure Varies

Although we know there are high concentrations of pollutants close to major roadways, it's harder to measure an individual's exposure because of where and when activities take place. Indoor pollutant concentrations are mediated by numerous factors including a building's ventilation and pollutant decay rates; in-vehicle concentrations are related to the exhaust of vehicles in front and to traffic densities. Individual exposure is also determined by activity level and breathing rate. For instance, young children have high breathing rates and therefore inhale a relatively larger volume of pollutants than older children or adults. Even a part of the day spent playing outdoors downwind of a major roadway could comprise a significant proportion of a child's overall daily exposure to air pollution, given the higher rate of inhalation during moderate or vigorous play.

FAST FACT

Hybrid electric vehicles are 30–40 percent more gasoline-efficient than traditional gas-powered vehicles.

These factors are important for understanding the magnitude of health risks near major roadways and for developing appropriate policy responses and strategies to mitigate them. Because direct measurement of pollutant levels and individual exposure is expensive and difficult, researchers are learning to model individual- and neighborhood-level exposures to air pollutants to understand how they are affected by time of day, activity, and travel patterns. . . .

Concentrated Diesel Pollutants

Recent and projected expansions of goods movement corridors in Southern California raise many environmental justice concerns, including the potential localized effect of diesel pollution. Heavy-duty diesel trucks emit high levels of ultrafine and fine particles, and a complex mixture of gaseous air pollutants, 41 of which are listed by the State of California as toxic air contaminants. Transportation corridors with heavy-duty diesel traffic such as the 710 freeway in Los Angeles tend to have higher concentrations of these harmful pollutants than a freeway with less diesel traffic such as the 405. The California Department of Transportation says that in 2002 the segment of the 710 from the Ports of Long Beach and Los Angeles through the low-income, minority communities of Lynwood, South Gate, and Bell into East Los Angeles carried over 32,000 trucks per day, comprising up to fifteen percent of all the traffic on this segment. Much of this truck traffic carries goods throughout the entire region. According to the South Coast Air Quality District, diesel particulate emissions are responsible for about seventy percent of the estimated carcinogenic risk from air toxins. Although the expansion of goods movement corridors offers regional and national economic benefits, the cumulative local health effects of diesel exhaust might be huge. Near-roadway exposure to diesel-related pollutants such as ultrafine particles, black carbon, and carbon monoxide could also be compounded by nearby rail and port activities.

Reducing Emissions

Given the pervasiveness and necessity of urban roadways, multiple strategies will be required to address the adverse impacts of vehicle-related pollutants, especially since technological solutions for future gains in emission reduction appear limited in the near future. While gasoline vehicles have become much cleaner, on- and off-road heavy-duty diesel engines are just now being required to meet stricter emissions standards. Until recently, pollution controls on these engines were limited by the high sulfur content of diesel fuel. On-road diesel engine models of 2007 or newer sold in the United States will now be equipped with advanced pollution control technology such as particulate filters and required to use newly available ultra-low sulfur diesel fuel (ULSD). Similar requirements will be phased in over the next decade for new non-road diesel engines such as in construction, agricultural, and industrial equipment. The California Air Resources Board (ARB) suggests these new on-road diesel standards could result in a ninety percent reduction of NO_X emissions and a ninety percent reduction in particulate matter emissions compared to 2004 diesel standards.

Diesel engines are very durable, however, and can last for thirty years, which limits the near-term effectiveness of the new standards. Even though retrofitting older diesels with new emissions controls and using ULSD could help curb emissions, implementing a large-scale retrofit program is extremely challenging. The San Pedro Bay Ports recently proposed incentive programs to promote the replacement and retrofit of older heavy-duty diesels and to make alternate fuels and clean diesel more widely available.

Restricting Land Use

Another strategy restricts "sensitive land uses" away from major roadways. In 2003, the California legislature responded to the evidence of high concentrations of harmful pollutants near major roadways by prohibiting the construction of public schools within 500 feet of busy roadways. Ten percent of California public schools and nineteen percent of the state's licensed childcare centers are located within 500 feet of a major roadway. As many as 25 percent of childcare centers are located within 650 feet of a major roadway.

The California Air Resources Board recently developed recommendations for restricting residences, schools, day-care centers, playgrounds, and medical facilities near heavily traveled roadways and other air pollution sources. The board's objective is to reduce cumulative exposure from multiple sources of pollution—not just major roadways, but also sources such as distribution centers, rail yards, ports, refineries, and chrome platers. Similar proximity-based standards should become an integral part of the environmental review of transportation projects, regional transportation planning, and local land use planning.

With the recent adoption of new rules by the Environmental Protection Agency and the Federal Highway Administration, regional agencies will soon be required to demonstrate that transportation projects involving significant increases in diesel traffic (such as road expansions and new bus terminals) do not create hazardous hotspots of particulate matter. Initial guidelines for hotspot analysis include qualitative review and comparisons with similar projects in the region

Toxic Emissions from Motor Vehicles

Air pollution from motor vehicles is the result of fuel burning in the engine. Harmful chemicals are produced during this combustion process and released as exhaust. These chemicals cause a variety of human and environmental health problems.

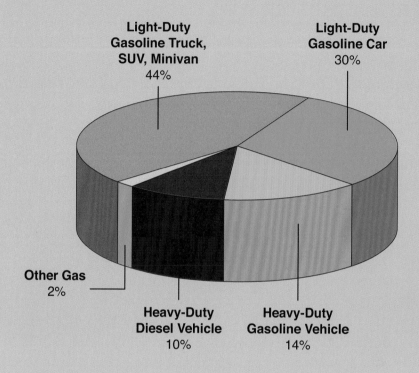

Light-Duty Gasoline Truck, SUV, Minivan
44%

Light-Duty Gasoline Car
30%

Other Gas
2%

Heavy-Duty Diesel Vehicle
10%

Heavy-Duty Gasoline Vehicle
14%

Taken from: Maine Department of Environmental Protection, Bureau of Air Quality, 2005.

to identify potential impacts. This new requirement could be a step in the right direction, but since it is just now being translated into practice and lacks clear guidelines for impact assessment, it remains unclear how effective it will prove.

Multiple Strategies Should Be Explored

A large-scale re-siting of sensitive land uses away from major roadways is highly unlikely. Therefore, multiple strategies should be explored to reduce exposures and protect public health. Further research is needed to better understand how vehicle-related pollutants disperse immediately adjacent to major roadways, and to study the extent to which barriers such as sound walls or landscape buffers can mediate the concentration of pollutants. Potential solutions may include the installation of air filtration systems in near-roadway facilities and residences to limit the intrusion of outdoor air. Strategic site design could help reduce the exposure of vulnerable populations to vehicle pollutants. For instance, playgrounds and outdoor activities at schools could be located on the side of the property farthest from major roadways. Outdoor and vigorous activities could be restricted during high traffic periods.

We're only beginning to understand the public health, policy, and societal implications of on- and near-roadway exposures to vehicle-related pollutants. . . . The integration of local-level concerns into regional transportation, air quality, land use, and growth planning is a daunting but worthwhile pursuit. We must localize the scale of our thinking even as we work towards regional prosperity and health.

EVALUATING THE AUTHORS' ARGUMENTS:

In this viewpoint Houston, Wu, Ong, and Winer offer several solutions to combat the dangerous health effects from vehicle pollutants. Describe each of these solutions. Then, explain whether you think they are practical. Is there a solution you feel strongly in favor of or against? Finally, suggest a solution to vehicle-related health problems not put forth by the authors.

Viewpoint 6

Gas-Powered Vehicles Burn Cleaner than Ever

Evan Griffey

"Auto manufacturers have developed a slew of technologies that have elevated the conventional gasoline engine to new heights in efficiency so buyers . . . can go green on gasoline."

In the following viewpoint Evan Griffey argues that gas-powered vehicles burn cleaner than ever and do not threaten the environment or human health the way older car models did. Modern gasoline-powered vehicles, says Griffey, have been built with technologies that allow for greater fuel efficiency and a significant reduction in emissions output. These advances put gas-powered cars in direct competition with hybrid vehicles, which are also environmentally friendly but cost much more. Griffey concludes that gasoline-powered cars are significantly cheaper than hybrid vehicles while offering comparable fuel economy and emissions performance.

Griffey is a writer whose articles have appeared in *Import Tuner, Sport Compact Car, Honda Tuning, Turbo & High Tech Performance, Car Audio,* and *Siphon* magazines. Previously Griffey spent thirteen years as an editor of *Turbo & High Tech Performance* magazine.

Evan Griffey, "Go Green with Gasoline," *www.autos.msn.com*, 2007. Reproduced by permission of MSN.

With global warming becoming widely accepted as fact, even by the likes of Congress, environmental consciousness is moving concerns such as emissions and fuel economy up the criteria list of many new-car buyers. While hybrid prices have come down in recent years, the cost difference between gas-electrics and conventional gasoline-powered vehicles is still the great divide in the hybrid/gasoline debate. But making the green choice does not necessarily mean driving a hybrid.

Go Green on Gasoline

Auto manufacturers have developed a slew of technologies that have elevated the conventional gasoline engine to new heights in efficiency so buyers concerned with the environmental impact can go green on gasoline.

More precise engine control computers and related programming coupled with refinements in injector design that provide more efficient spray patterns empower today's gasoline engines to burn fuel more completely than ever. On the post-combustion side, improvements in catalytic converter technology ensure any byproducts still in the system are thoroughly filtered.

How Emissions Are Rated

The Environmental Protection Agency (EPA) is not at the forefront of emissions ratings; California provides these benchmarks. Emissions efficiency of motor vehicles is measured at the tailpipe in particulate matter.

But there is also a secondary form of emissions: evaporative emissions that escape into the air in the form of fumes. This kind of emission usually occurs during fill-up at the gas station, but also takes place by way of venting from the fuel tank—vaporization of the fuel when the engine is running and heat soak after the car is parked. Depending on the vehicle, evaporative emissions can rival that of tailpipe emissions on hot days when the evaporation threshold is lowered.

California's Air Resources Board (CARB) rates its emissions with catchy acronyms while the EPA's rating system uses a zero to ten scale in its "Guide To Green Cars" that allows direct comparisons between different model groups, i.e., compact cars and light trucks. Since California has more stringent emissions criteria and the car companies sell a great deal of cars there, the catchy acronyms get all the attention.

PZEV Vehicles Can Compete with Hybrids

According to the Golden State [California], ZEV or Zero Emission Vehicles have zero tailpipe emissions and are 98-percent cleaner than the average new model year vehicle. Only all-electric and fuel-cell vehicles can gain entrance into the ZEV category.

AT-PZEV or Advanced Technology Partial Zero Emission Vehicles meet SULEV (see below) tailpipe emission standards, carry a 15-year/150,000-mile warranty and have zero evaporative emissions. The Advanced Technology part of the term refers to components such as gas-electric hybrids or compressed natural gas vehicles, but not plain gasoline-powered vehicles.

The best a gasoline-powered car can aspire to is a PZEV or Partial Zero Emission Vehicles rating. Like AT-PZEVs these vehicles also meet SULEV tailpipe emission standards, have a 15-year/150,000-mile warranty and have zero evaporative emissions.

The difference between AT-PZEV and PZEV is PZEVs have no electric or other hybrid drive system. Many PZEV vehicles are sold in the states of California, Massachusetts, New York, Vermont and Maine as standard and required equipment and may be available as an option in bordering states.

> **FAST FACT**
>
> Modern gas-powered cars burn so cleanly, a conventional lawn mower pollutes as much in an hour as forty late-model cars (or as much air pollution as driving a car for one hundred miles).

Gasoline-Powered Cars Are Better than Most Alternatives

It takes five barrels of crude oil to produce enough gasoline (nearly 97 gal.) to power a Honda Civic from New York to California. Most alternatives to gas-powered engines are more expensive, or use gas themselves.

Car	Raw Materials Consumed	Fuel Needed	Fuel Cost	Price	Economy	Fuel Type
2006 Honda Civic	4.5 barrels of crude oil	90.9 Gallons	$212.70	$2.34/ Gal	33 MPG	Gasoline: Honda Civic is the benchmark for all the vehicles in this virtual comparison. It burns regular 87-octane gasoline (available on every corner), even if it's not always cheap.
2005 Taurus FFV	53 bushels of corn and a half-barrel of crude oil	176 Gallons	$425.00	$2.41/ Gal	17 MPG	E85/Ethanol: Current Taurus FFV burns 85% ethanol and 15% gasoline (The gas gets the engine started on cold days.) This mix provides about 15% less mileage than straight gasoline, but burns cleanly and reduces pollution.
1998 Taurus M85 FFV	18,190 cu. ft. of natural gas and a half-barrel of crude oil	214 Gallons	$619.00	$2.89/ Gal	14 MPG	M85/Methanol: Mid-'90s Taurus FFV ran on M85 sold in California in a limited number of stations, and also to some dedicated fleets. Low BTU content of methanol means 35% fewer miles per gallon. Made from natural gas, methanol burns cleanly.
2006 Golf TDI	16.5-gallon jugs of used vegetable oil	68.2 Gallons	$231.00	$3.40/ Gal	44 MPG	B100 Biodiesel: VW Golf and new Beetle TDI are the mileage champs of all conventional cars, sipping diesel fuel at a miserly rate. (And they can burn B100, although VW only recommends B5.) B20 would lower the cost of the trip to less than $183.
2005 Civic GX	10,650 cu. ft. of natural gas	88 GGE*	$110.00	$1.25/ GGE	34 MPGGE	Compressed Natural Gas: Honda Civic GX can be refueled at home—as could any CNG vehicle—with a home compressor. But crossing the country in a dedicated CNG car would be tough: There aren't a lot of CNG stations, and many are for fleet use only.
1997 Honda EV Plus	About 1 ton of coal	16.4 GGE	$60.00	$3.66/ GGE	202 MPGGE	Electricity: Late-'90s Honda EV Plus got about 100 highway miles on a nearly full charge of 20 kilowatt-hours (kwh). The vehicle's NIMH battery pack had a total capacity of 26.5 kwh. Electrics do better in traffic, thanks to regenerative braking.
GM Hy-Wire	16,000 cu. ft. of hydrogen	73 GGE	$804.00	$11/ GGE	41 MPGGE	Hydrogen Fuel Cell: Hy-Wire concept uses compressed hydrogen, which costs about four times as much as gasoline, although the DOE projects prices below $2/GGE by 2012. New technology will double vehicle range by raising tank pressure to 10,000 psi.

*GGE stands for Gallon of Gas Equivalent.

Taken from: *Popular Mechanics*, 2006.

SULEV or Super Ultra Low Emission Vehicles operate 90-percent cleaner than the average new model year vehicle. The difference between SULEV and PZEV ratings is the lack of evaporative emissions and warranty requirements. ULEV or Ultra Low Emission Vehicles are 50-percent cleaner than the average new model year vehicle.

The last of these alphabetical tongue twisters is LEV or Low Emission Vehicles, which represent the lowest emissions standard for all new cars sold in California. Think of it as extra credit for being significantly cleaner than the EPA minimum.

The EPA's new scale shows two points of measurement; an air pollution rating and a greenhouse gas rating. Vehicles in the PZEV category mostly score 9.5 with a few 9s. The same make and model car in below-PZEV trim that are sold in states other than California, Massachusetts, New York, Vermont and Maine score 8s and 9s.

Fuel Economy Is Difficult to Determine

The second environmental concern for the new-car buyer is fuel economy. The benefits of good fuel economy are the use of less gasoline and saving all the resources that go into creating said gasoline. The owner also pays less money for fuel over the lifetime of the car. Fuel mileage is where the biggest difference between hybrid and gasoline-powered offerings arises.

However, with wildly fluctuating gas prices it can be difficult to put a real price tag on the savings. Since hybrids run on electricity more in the city and gasoline-powered cars are less efficient in slow-and-go city traffic, hybrids show the greatest advantage when city MPG is compared.

Gas-Powered Vehicles Are More Cost-Effective

Looking at the vehicle comparison, a significant trend jumps into the light—overall value. Cost-wise the average of the top three hybrids checks in at $23,658. Working the same equations with the top three gas-powered cars nets a bottom line of $13,101. The difference of $10,557 really wallops the wallet. (It should be noted that all prices are for the base model vehicle with no optional equipment added.) So whether mileage or emissions output is the driving force behind the purchase decision the great divide tops $10,000.

From a fuel efficiency standpoint the Toyota Yaris is the standout because it delivers the best city MPG, 40 MPG on the highway (one MPG off the best score), ULEV emissions performance and does it with the lowest price on the road, $11,150.

Focusing in on emissions as the deciding factor, the Ford Focus moves to the top of the chart. It combines a SULEV engine with zero evaporative emissions and delivers 27/37 mileage, the best of the PZEVs, and does so at just over $14,000.

Comparing Hybrids and Non-hybrids

The Toyota Prius puts up the best numbers because there are far less compromises in a vehicle designed from conception as a hybrid than in an existing platform that is converted into a hybrid. In some ways examining the gasoline and hybrid versions of the same car under the same microscope better frames the hybrid/gas proposition.

Accord and Accord Hybrid are equal in emissions and the one and two-MPG improvements cost a staggering $12,465.

We see the big advantage hybrids have in the city—16 MPG more than the non-hybrid Camry. Those with freeway-dominated commutes will only see a 4 MPG bump. Again emissions is a wash as both vehicles are at the top of the scale. The price difference is $7,730.

The Honda Civic gas-versus-hybrid comparison shows the biggest gap in fuel efficiency and emissions. A PZEV rating is better than 90 percent of all cars while a ULEV rating beats only 50 percent. The price difference is $7,790.

PZEVs Burn Clean

Gasoline-burning PZEV cars are a cost-effective way to drive clean. How clean? On a smoggy day, or even a not-so-smoggy day, in downtown Los Angeles the emissions coming from a PZEV tailpipe will be cleaner than the air outside. Further, grilling a hamburger on the BBQ would produce more hydrocarbon emissions than a PZEV would on a three-hour trip (180 miles). In fact, PZEVs can burn cleaner than some hybrids when the hybrids' gasoline engine does not meet SULEV standards.

The most prolific PZEV is the Ford Focus with more than 100,000 of the DURATEC 20E-powered cars on the road since 2003. Ford

Hybrid cars like the Toyota Prius provide cleaner emissions but their high price tag makes them prohibitively expensive for most consumers.

recently began badging PZEV Focuses with a Green Leaf Highway emblem to enhance awareness because, according to Ford, many owners may not realize the environmental significance of their car.

Geography can be conspiring against eco-conscious buyers. The PZEV's limited availability is not a result of sales volume, marketing or any other political force; it's all about fuel quality. The reformulated fuel available in what's called the California Emission States—California, Massachusetts, New York, Vermont and Maine—make PZEV possible. Take a PZEV to Kansas and the change in fuel quality will knock down its emissions performance. Many PZEVs like the Ford Focus may be available in states bordering the California Emission States but in the case of Ford the 130-hp DURATEC 20E engine is a no-cost option.

For those living on the right side of the tracks the availability of gasoline cars that deliver PZEV emissions performance and outstanding fuel economy make living a green life much more affordable compared to going hybrid. Those without PZEV can still get significant emissions performance, competitive mileage and go easy on the environment while reaping 5-figure cost savings. The key is to be well informed and know what you want before waltzing into the local dealership, be it down the street or in cyber space.

EVALUATING THE AUTHOR'S ARGUMENTS:

The author of this viewpoint, Evan Griffey, has spent many years editing articles for car magazines. Do you consider him qualified to write on this topic? Why or why not? Do the author's credentials influence your opinion of his argument? In what way?

Chapter 3

Should Oil Be Replaced with Other Energy Sources?

The debate over alternative energy has sparked controversy over which sources would be the best to pursue.

Viewpoint

1

Oil Should Be Replaced with Nuclear Power

Kevin Bullis

"We who live in the nuclear age are approaching a crossroads, a moment of truth. . . . The benefits of nuclear energy are needed [now] more than ever."

In the following viewpoint author Kevin Bullis speaks with specialists who argue that nuclear power could provide a clean, inexpensive source of energy to meet growing demand in poor nations. They describe how small nuclear power plants could be built to serve individual towns while limiting the potential for reactor meltdowns or threats from terrorists trying to acquire nuclear materials.

Kevin Bullis is the nanotechnology and materials science editor for *Technology Review*, a publication of the Massachusetts Institute of Technology.

AS YOU READ, CONSIDER THE FOLLOWING QUESTIONS:

1. By what percentage will carbon dioxide emissions increase in the next 25 years according to Mohamed ElBaradei?
2. According to the speakers what safeguards would help prevent nuclear proliferation?
3. What arguments do the speakers use to describe the cost savings that would come from building small nuclear power plants?

Kevin Bullis, "Small Nuclear Self-Contained Power Plants Could Supply Growing Energy Demand in Poor Countries," *Technology Review*, November 10, 2005. Copyright © 2005 by the Association of Alumni and Alumnae of MIT. Reproduced by permission.

Now more than ever, the world needs nuclear energy, says this year's Nobel Peace Prize laureate, Mohamed ElBaradei. In a talk at MIT last week he cited a new report from the International Energy Agency that said world energy demand will increase by 50 percent in the next 25 years. Meanwhile, carbon dioxide emissions, which are a leading cause of global warming, will increase by the same percentage. Nuclear power could provide a significant amount of that power, without producing the carbon dioxide, says ElBaradei.

It's an argument that's attracting more and more proponents these days. But traditional nuclear power plants are very expensive to build, which can be a serious obstacle to their construction in poor countries. One solution being proposed, according to ElBaradei, is to build hundreds of small nuclear power plants, each designed to serve a single town. Such plants could be built for a fraction of the cost of the current large-scale regional ones. And they could be installed without the need to also build an extensive and expensive power grid. As a country's energy needs grow, more plants can be added to keep up. Such plants might also be a good solution for remote communities.

> **FAST FACT**
>
> Surveys show that Americans are misinformed about nuclear power. One survey found that just 16.9 percent of Americans knew that no one was killed in the Three Mile Island meltdown incident in 1979. More than 38 percent of Americans believed people had died in the accident.

Safeguarding Small Nuclear Plants

A countryside dotted with hundreds of small reactors might seem like a safety and nuclear proliferation nightmare. But, according to ElBaradei, director general of the International Atomic Energy Agency, they can be built with safeguards against meltdowns and theft of materials by would-be terrorists.

Researchers at Argonne National Laboratory in Argonne, IL, described a concept for such a small-scale reactor this summer. One of the safeguards is a passive cooling system, which continues to work even if power goes down. The reactors could also operate for 30 years

Nuclear Power Is a Cost-Effective Energy Source

At $1.72 per kilowatt-hour, nuclear power is one of the least expensive energy sources.

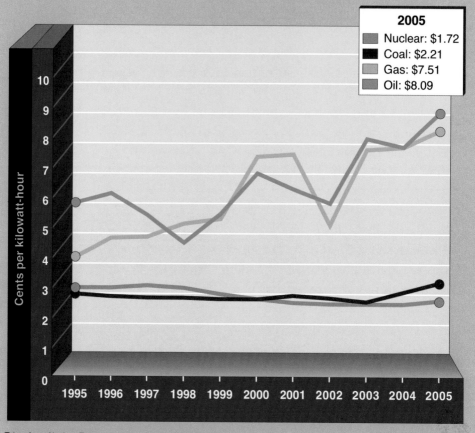

2005
- Nuclear: $1.72
- Coal: $2.21
- Gas: $7.51
- Oil: $8.09

Cents per kilowatt-hour

1995 1996 1997 1998 1999 2000 2001 2002 2003 2004 2005

Taken from: Nuclear Energy, 2006. www.uic.com/au/nip08.htm.

without refueling, which would mean fewer deliveries that could be hijacked. And stealing the fuel while it was in the reactor would require bringing to the site extensive heavy equipment, which would be easily visible by satellite, according to David Wade, senior technical advisor at Argonne and one of the developers of the concept.

"It's good to have a reactor that requires a minimum of maintenance and refueling" for remote locations in some situations, says Mujid Kazimi, a nuclear engineer at MIT. He says that similar small reactors are under development in Argentina and Brazil, and Toshiba has recently offered to build one for an Alaskan town.

Keeping the Reactor Cool

The Argonne concept uses a reactor cooled by liquid lead that allows for high operating temperatures and efficient use of the fuel, which is programmed to produce energy slowly over the 30-year cycle. The lead coolant also circulates without the need for the expensive back-up diesel generators required by today's plants. "If it is built correctly, it will be able to be cooled by natural convection alone," says Kazimi, who was not part of the concept development team.

The power plant would be mostly buried underground for protection, and surrounded by a back-up passive air cooling system–hot air rises out of the exhaust stack and cool air is pulled in through low vents. This system would run continuously, essentially wasting about one percent of the heat generated, yet ensuring that the reactor would cool off in the case of a problem.

The reactor is partially self-regulating. If the temperature rises, the structures containing the fuel expand, causing the fuel to spread out, and slowing down the frequency of the neutron collisions that create the nuclear reaction. This, in turn, causes the temperature to fall. These features, says Wade, should simplify the control of the plant and prevent meltdowns.

France has led the world in developing nuclear power. Here is a model of a facility that developers believe will provide clean, inexhaustible, and safe power.

The lead will also serve as a safety measure. The fuel will be delivered inside the lead in a solid form, to be melted on site. When this module is removed and replaced after thirty years, the lead will cool off—now encasing the used fuel. This can be returned to a central facility for reprocessing, after which almost all of the spent fuel can be reused, says Wade.

Mass-Producing Reactors

On the downside, building small reactors means losing out on the economy of scale that has driven a trend toward bigger and bigger reactors, says Wade. He hopes to make up for this by creating ways to mass-produce the reactors in modules that can be quickly assembled on site.

For Wade, small reactors are part of a vision for large-scale changes. "What we're trying to do is not only change the technology, but also exploit it, by changing the infrastructures. You can ship thirty years of energy with a single core loading, to provide energy security for a country without the need to install the infrastructure [for processing the fuel] right on its own territory." ElBaradei says designs such as the one developed at Argonne could actually "reduce access to sensitive nuclear material" if countries agreed to share fuel facilities. "We cannot afford to have every country sitting on an enrichment factory or reprocessing facility," he says. If a country with such a facility begins to feel threatened, it "would be able to develop nuclear weapons within a matter of months."

"We who live in the nuclear age are approaching a crossroads, a moment of truth," ElBaradei told the audience at MIT. "Will this technology continue to be harnessed as a servant of development? Or will we become the victim of its destructive power?" For now, he says, "the benefits of nuclear energy are needed more than ever."

EVALUATING THE AUTHORS' ARGUMENTS:

Kevin Bullis's article claims that nuclear power is a safe and inexpensive power source. How do you think the author of the following viewpoint, Jim Green, would respond to this claim? With what evidence might he dispute it? Be specific in your answer.

Oil Should Not Be Replaced with Nuclear Power

Jim Green

"The replacement of all fossil fuel fired electricity plants with nuclear power would be unlikely to reduce global greenhouse emissions by more than 5-10%."

In the following viewpoint Jim Green argues that nuclear power is an impractical, dangerous energy source that should not replace oil. Green states that in order to replace the amount of electricity generated by fossil fuels with nuclear power, the world would need to build thousands of new reactors. These reactors would pose several problems: for one, they produce dangerous radioactive waste. Secondly, their nuclear materials would be vulnerable to terrorists and rogue states that seek weapons of mass destruction. For these reasons, Green concludes that human safety and environmental risks outweigh any potential benefit nuclear power might offer as an alternative to oil.

Jim Green is an antinuclear campaigner with Friends of the Earth, an international network of environmental organizations that works to defend the environment and promote a just world.

Jim Green, "Global Warming: Nuclear Power No Solution," *www.greenleft.org*, April 13, 2005. Reproduced by permission of the author.

AS YOU READ, CONSIDER THE FOLLOWING QUESTIONS:
1. How many countries have used their nuclear reactors for non-peaceful purposes, according to the author?
2. How many nuclear reactors would be required to replace all energy derived from fossil fuels, according to the author?
3. Why does the author say nuclear power cannot be considered a "green" energy source?

Have the nuclear industry and its supporters suddenly gained an environmental consciousness? While they're not planning to close their dangerous, polluting reactors nor begin dealing responsibly with their legacy of toxic radioactive wastes, they are now professing deep concern about climate change—and argue that nuclear power is the only solution.

Even environmentalists are turning to nuclear power, we're told. It's not true—you could count them on one hand—but the nuclear boosters and the mainstream media aren't letting the facts get in the way of a good story.

Proponents of nuclear power downplay or ignore altogether the problems that would be exacerbated by an expansion of nuclear power globally or the introduction of nuclear power into Australia—including nuclear weapons proliferation, radioactive waste, and the risk of catastrophic accidents.

Nuclear Weapons Proliferation

The "peaceful" nuclear power and research sectors have produced enough fissile material to build over 110,000 nuclear weapons. Australian uranium has resulted in the production of more than 60 [metric] tons of plutonium, sufficient to produce about 6000 nuclear weapons.

Supposedly "peaceful" nuclear facilities can be—and have been—used in various ways for weapons research and production. Of the 60 countries which have built nuclear power or research reactors, about 25 are known to have used their "peaceful" nuclear facilities for covert weapons research and/or production—a strike rate of about 40%.

Israel, India, Pakistan, South Africa and possibly North Korea have succeeded in producing nuclear weapons under cover of a "peaceful" nuclear program.

Claims that the international safeguards system prevents misuse of "peaceful" nuclear facilities and materials are grossly overstated. Recent statements from the UN's International Atomic Energy Agency and US President George [W.] Bush about the need to limit the spread of enrichment and reprocessing technology, and to establish multinational control over sensitive nuclear facilities, amount to an acknowledgement of the fundamental flaws of the international safeguards system.

Retired Australian diplomat Professor Richard Broinowski notes in his 2003 book *Fact or Fission? The Truth About Australia's Nuclear Ambitions* that accounting for Australian uranium exports is "tenuous, and subject to distortion or abuse."

Radioactive Waste Poses an Environmental Threat

Not a single repository exists for the disposal of high-level radioactive waste, which is produced at an annual rate of about 10,000 [metric] tons in nuclear power reactors worldwide. Technologies exist to encapsulate or immobilize radionuclides to a greater or lesser degree, but encapsulated radioactive waste still represents a potential public health and environmental threat that will last for millennia.

The prospects for transmutation—using neutrons or charged particle beams to convert longer-lived radionuclides into shorter-lived radionuclides or stable isotopes—are grim for a number of reasons.

Reprocessing spent reactor fuel is polluting, and most of the uranium and plutonium arising from reprocessing is simply stockpiled with no plans for its use. Separation of plutonium from spent fuel poses a major proliferation risk—many tons of plutonium are stockpiled, and a typical 1000 megawatt electric (MWe) reactor produces about 300 kilograms of plutonium each year, enough to produce about 30 nuclear weapons.

More Reactors Mean More Accidents

The more reactors, the more accidents. The more accidents, the more likely significant off-site releases of radioactivity. The "new generation of passively safe reactors" face various obstacles, such as not being new or passively safe! For example, so-called pebble-bed reactor technology is a variation on the theme of high temperature reactors, which have been investigated by many countries, abandoned in most, and successful in none.

FAST FACT

Forty percent of countries that have claimed their nuclear facilities were for peaceful purposes have instead used them for military means.

In addition to the perennial problems of plant malfunction and human error, terrorism looms large as a threat to nuclear plants and everyone working and living in their vicinity.

Nuclear power proponents deny the likelihood that the 1986 Chernobyl disaster has killed thousands and will kill thousands more. They do this by hiding behind the complexities of epidemiological studies and using those complexities to obfuscate. However, using the standard risk estimates applied the world over, the likely toll from Chernobyl will be some tens of thousands of deaths.

Nuclear Power Is Not a Solution

The world's 440 operating power reactors, with about 364,000 MWe of total capacity, produce about 16% of the world's electricity. Coal, gas and oil account for four times that amount—about 64%. So to replace fossil fuel generated electricity with nuclear power would require a five-fold increase in the number of reactors, from 440 to about 2200. The cost of the additional 1760 reactors would be several *trillion* dollars.

The 2200 reactors would produce enough plutonium each year to build roughly 60,000 nuclear weapons. The annual production of high-level radioactive waste in the form of spent fuel would increase to about 50,000 [metric] tons—to be safely and securely stored in those repositories that don't exist.

But what of the benefits of closing all those fossil fuel fired plants? Electricity generation is responsible for only a modest percentage of global greenhouse gas emissions—as low as 9% by some accounts. In broad terms the replacement of all fossil fuel fired electricity plants with nuclear power would be unlikely to reduce global greenhouse emissions by more than 5-10%—not even close to the 60% reduction required to stabilize atmospheric concentrations of greenhouse gases.

It is theoretically possible that nuclear power could be used not only for electricity production but also for other purposes such as producing hydrogen for transportation. However, that would just make the task all the more impractical and all the more alarming in terms of proliferation risks and radioactive waste production. According to [socialist and writer] John Busby, about 200 nuclear reactors would be required in Australia alone to produce both electricity and hydrogen for transportation.

Environmental activists question the safety of nuclear power as they protest plans to build more nuclear reactors in France.

No Government or Public Support

In Australia, building nuclear reactors would not only be irresponsible and impractical as a means of addressing climate change, it would also be illegal because the Howard government [led by Prime Minister John Howard] outlawed the construction of nuclear power reactors in the 1998 Australian Radiation Protection and Nuclear Safety Act. Interestingly, the government made nuclear power illegal with little or no prompting from environmental and anti-nuclear groups.

Even if a future government attempted to push ahead with construction of nuclear power reactors, the public opposition would be immense. The only serious proposal to build a nuclear power plant in Australia—at Jervis Bay in NSW in the late 1960s—was defeated by public and political opposition. The Jervis Bay project was driven by then-Coalition PM [Prime Minister] John Gorton, who later admitted that the intention was not only to produce electricity but also to produce plutonium for nuclear weapons.

Nuclear Plants Produce Greenhouse Gases

Claims that nuclear power is "greenhouse free" are nonsense. Substantial greenhouse gas generation occurs across the nuclear fuel cycle. Nonetheless, fossil fuel derived electricity is considerably more greenhouse intensive—for the moment.

Emissions per unit energy from nuclear power are about one third of those from large gas-fired electricity plants. However, this comparative benefit of nuclear power is substantially eroded, and eventually negated altogether, as higher-grade uranium ores are depleted and lower-grade ores are mined. Most of the Earth's uranium is found in very poor grade ores. That trend would of course be hastened in a scenario in which nuclear power replaces large numbers of fossil fuel fired electricity plants.

Even at the current rate of consumption, low-cost uranium reserves will be exhausted in about 50 years according to John Carlson from the Australian Safeguards and Non-proliferation Office, the disgraceful nuclear regulatory agency which acts more like a pro-nuclear PR agency.

At this point in the argument, nuclear boosters such as Carlson pull out their trump card—the wondrous plutonium economy in which fast breeder reactors produce more plutonium fuel than they consume—and nuclear power may yet be too cheap to meter! However, most plutonium breeder R&D programs have been abandoned because of technical, economic and safety problems. In any case, the weapons proliferation risks of a plutonium economy are totally unacceptable. Nuclear fusion also poses proliferation risks, and faces seemingly insurmountable technical and economic problems.

EVALUATING THE AUTHORS' ARGUMENTS:

Jim Green describes threats—like weapons proliferation and accidents—that can develop from "peaceful" nuclear programs. Kevin Bullis, author of the previous viewpoint, also presents perspectives on these threats. What would the speakers in Bullis's article think of Green's description? Explain using evidence from the text. After reading both viewpoints, what is your opinion on whether nuclear power should replace oil as an energy source?

Viewpoint

3

Oil Should Be Replaced with Wind Power

Mark Lambrides and Juan Cruz Monticelli

"Wind does not generate local pollution or result in emissions that cause climate change."

In the following viewpoint Mark Lambrides and Juan Cruz Monticelli argue that energy generated by oil should be replaced with wind power. They explain that in order to reduce oil imports, many countries have had success building high-tech wind farms that harness the power of wind and convert it into enough electricity to supply individual homes or even entire towns. The authors say these wind farms are increasingly efficient and cost effective. In addition, wind energy is a renewable resource that will not be depleted like fossil fuels, and as such can provide a long-lasting solution to reducing the world's dependence on oil. Furthermore, wind power can be generated domestically, solving the problem of America's dependence on foreign sources for its energy. For all these reasons, the authors suggest wind power should replace oil as a dominant energy source in the United States.

Lambrides is the energy and climate change division chief and Monticelli is a lawyer and energy specialist at the Organization of American States Department of Sustainable Development.

Mark Lambrides and Juan Cruz Monticelli, "Illuminating the Power of Renewable Energy," *Americas.* Reproduced by permission of Organization of American States.

AS YOU READ, CONSIDER THE FOLLOWING QUESTIONS:

1. How many households does the Caribbean's Wigton Wind Farm provide power to each year?
2. What were windmills used for in Persia between the sixth and tenth centuries, according to the authors?
3. In the past eight years the average cost of electricity produced at a 20 megawatt wind farm has decreased by how much, according to the authors?

In Wigton, 71 miles east of Kingston, the capital of Jamaica, there is a farm. It's not your average, ordinary farm, however. If you go there, you won't find a farmer in overalls, or ploughs and tractors, or a stable, or cows and chickens. This farm produces something invisible that is distributed throughout the country, not by trucks, but via power lines. It produces electricity.

Converting Wind to Electricity

Twenty-three wind powered generators, each 160 feet high, stand in the fields of Wigton, 2,300 feet above sea level. Each turbine is equipped with enormous blades more than 170 feet in diameter. The turbines convert the kinetic energy of air currents—wind—into electricity. Temperature and pressure changes produced in the atmosphere by the absorption of the sun's rays make the air move naturally from high pressure areas to low pressure areas, and this air movement creates wind. This process is particularly notable in the Caribbean, where the "trade winds" blow frequently and powerfully.

With an installed capacity of 20.7 megawatts and connected to the country's electric grid, the Wigton Wind Farm is the largest in the Caribbean. In fact, the power it generates is enough to supply more than 25,000 households per year. To build it, the Jamaica Petroleum

> **FAST FACT**
>
> According to a survey published by the Manhattan Institute, 67.7 percent of Americans believe that renewable sources of energy are the safest to produce and use.

Wind farms have grown in number as they can be a good source of clean, renewable energy.

Corporation hired workers and young engineers from the area and trained them in wind energy technologies and substation management. In addition to the benefits of local jobs and clean electricity generated from domestic rather than imported fuels, the project supports a series of local economic and social activities, including support for the nearby rural school.

An Age-Old Idea

The Wigton Wind Farm has become an important model for other countries looking to convert wind into essential renewable energy by using the latest technologies. But this modern and innovative project is based on an age-old idea. In fact, humans have been harnessing the power of the wind to generate energy for thousands of years. Sails that used wind power to move boats were the first example. Later, rudimentary wind mills were built in Persia between the sixth and tenth centuries. These vertical axis machines were used to mill grain and pump water. Variations of this technology were created throughout the centuries until the advent of electricity.

To meet today's needs, however, the traditional wind mill has been redesigned, marrying aerospace and computer technologies to open a whole new generation of wind technologies. Modern wind mills can produce enough electricity to supply individual households or they can be multi-megawatt machines connected to large power grids.

Wind farms are now operating in more than 65 countries worldwide. In Latin America, the countries of Mexico, Costa Rica, Brazil, Argentina, and Ecuador are utilizing this valuable resource, along with other renewable energy sources, to help meet their energy needs.

The Many Benefits of Wind Power

Why is there now a growing emphasis on the use of renewable natural resources for energy generation? For Jamaica, the answer is clear. Wind does not generate local pollution or result in emissions that cause climate change. Wind is a local resource, so there is less need to import fuels. Finally, once the investment is made in a wind power plant, there is a reduced cost for fuel; so the price of power does not fluctuate drastically. These and other advantages are very attractive for a country whose energy generation otherwise depends almost exclusively on imported oil, and whose inhabitants pay more than 25 cents per kilowatt hour of electricity, more than four times what some energy users in the United States pay for the same service.

Modern renewable energy involves various kinds of power generation and fuel conversion processes that use inexhaustible or naturally

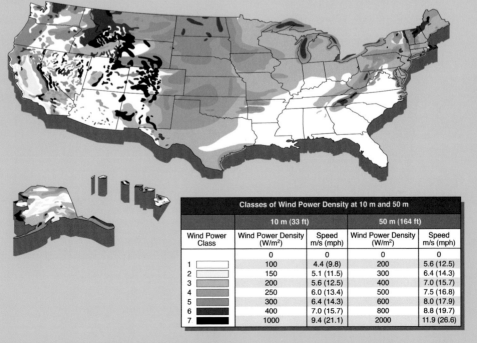

United States Annual Average Wind Power

The United States receives much wind that could be harnessed and used as an energy source.

	Classes of Wind Power Density at 10 m and 50 m			
	10 m (33 ft)		50 m (164 ft)	
Wind Power Class	Wind Power Density (W/m²)	Speed m/s (mph)	Wind Power Density (W/m²)	Speed m/s (mph)
	0	0	0	0
1	100	4.4 (9.8)	200	5.6 (12.5)
2	150	5.1 (11.5)	300	6.4 (14.3)
3	200	5.6 (12.5)	400	7.0 (15.7)
4	250	6.0 (13.4)	500	7.5 (16.8)
5	300	6.4 (14.3)	600	8.0 (17.9)
6	400	7.0 (15.7)	800	8.8 (19.7)
7	1000	9.4 (21.1)	2000	11.9 (26.6)

Taken from: United States National Renewable Energy Laboratory.

reproduced resources as fuel. Enormous technological developments during the last 30 years have resulted in huge improvements in the efficiency of these technologies and dramatic reductions in their costs. For example, the average cost of electricity generated at a 20 megawatt wind farm has fallen by over 25 percent in the past eight years. As a result, we are seeing an increase in the use of wind energy and expanding options available to customers. During the same period of time, the use of wind energy increased seven-fold around the world, from 10 gigawatts installed capacity to over 71 gigawatts. . . .

Wind Power Has Longevity

The production of sustainable energy is becoming more reliable, environmentally friendly, and cost effective, but its supply depends on a diversity of energy resources and proven technologies. No single source—renewable, fossil, or nuclear—will address all of the challenges. The environment, energy security, cost-effectiveness, and local job creation are among the many reasons why countries are seeking to increase their use of domestically sourced energy resources, including renewables. While it is true that no one can forecast exactly when fossil fuel reserves will run out on the planet, they will one day run out. Renewable energy—which before the use of fossil fuels was the only energy source used by human beings for more than 5,000 years—is now back to stay.

> **EVALUATING THE AUTHORS' ARGUMENTS:**
>
> In this viewpoint Lambrides and Monticelli describe the success of Jamaica's Wigton Wind Farm in utilizing wind power to produce energy. They argue the Wigton Wind Farm is a good model for other countries seeking to use alternative energy resources. In your opinion, is Wigton a good model? Do you think this type of wind farm would have the same results in other countries? Why or why not?

Viewpoint
4

Oil Should Not Be Replaced with Wind Power

Ed Hiserodt

"If wind power is so unreliable, doesn't replace power plants, and promises to have many siting restrictions, why would anyone support it?"

In the following viewpoint Ed Hiserodt argues that replacing oil with wind energy is costly and ineffective. In his opinion, replacing oil with renewable resources such as wind power is misguided and will cost taxpayers billions of dollars. Furthermore, wind turbines require large swaths of nature to be paved, hardly the mark of an environmentally friendly resource. Their potential to kill numerous birds and bats, and the inability of wind turbines to generate power when winds cease to blow, are other problems surrounding wind power. For these reasons, Hiserodt concludes that wind power will not replace oil as an efficient, environmentally friendly, or cost-effective energy source.

Hiserodt is an aerospace engineer and has been president of Controls & Power, Inc. since 1983. He is the author of *Underexposed: What If Radiation Is Actually GOOD for You?*

Ed Hiserodt, "Blown Away," *The New American,* September 3, 2007. Reproduced by permission.

AS YOU READ, CONSIDER THE FOLLOWING QUESTIONS:
1. How many square miles would need to be paved to build enough wind turbines to power Arkansas, according to the author?
2. Why would the United States be unable to get rid of its coal-fired power plants if it moved to wind power, according to Hiserodt?
3. In what three locations does the U.S. Fish and Wildlife Service not recommend installing wind turbines?

Hardly a stump speech goes by without a political candidate calling for "more renewable sources of energy such as wind or solar" to either stop our dependence on foreign oil or to slow the CO_2 emissions that mean certain doom for our planet. The politicians are doing what most politicians do: spewing rhetoric that they know voters want to hear; proposing programs they know little or nothing about.

Wind Energy Will Not Help

But as of August 3 [2007], the rhetoric was backed by action and the stakes became serious—as they say, "The price of poker just went up." On that day the U.S. House of Representatives voted to require electrical utilities to obtain 15 percent of their power from renewable sources. Since in some cases four percent of the renewable requirement could be satisfied by some "energy efficiency methods," this means that as "little" as 11 percent would need to come from renewable sources. The deadline for this conversion is 2020, with the threat of millions of dollars in penalties for those not meeting the requirement.

With only a Democrat-controlled Senate to temper the House bill, and a president who has shown a reluctance to veto terrible legislation, e.g., the Campaign Finance Law, the House bill represents a clear and present danger to the economy of the Republic—and will not lead to any reduction in our dependence on foreign oil or to any decrease in global warming.

Wind Cannot Provide Enough Electricity

To bring the scope of what is being proposed closer to home, let's use my home state, Arkansas, as a microcosm of the country as a whole. The State of Arkansas has almost exactly one percent of the U.S. population and is about midway in terms of area.

At a 2.2-percent growth rate in electrical consumption, the total for Arkansas in 2020 would be approximately 63 billion kilowatt hours (kWh) of electricity. As a comparison a 100-watt light bulb operating for a year (8,760 hours) would consume 876,000 watt-hours of power, or 876 kWh. Taking the lesser figure from the House Bill of 11 percent of "renewable" energy required, Arkansas utilities would be forced to provide 6.9 billion kWh from "renewable sources," which is clearly meant to be either wind or solar. . . .

Let's see what it will take to convert 11 percent of the electrical output to wind power. First we will have to estimate the capacity factor of a particular turbine generator used in an expected wind environment. Because of less-than-optimal wind speeds in all of Arkansas, the capacity factor would not be 30 percent but something in the neighborhood of five percent, but let us generously assign a 15-percent capacity factor to a 1,500 kW turbine with a blade diameter four-fifths the length of a football field. This one unit would produce 1,971,000 kWh of electricity over a year.

Remember how many kilowatt-hours we need for that 11 percent of *green* power? Yes, 6.9 billion. Dividing 6.9 billion by 1,971,000 gives us the number of wind turbine generators needed: 3,516.

> **FAST FACT**
>
> According to the Energy Information Administration, global demand for oil will increase by 37 percent by 2030. Whereas today demand is about 86 million barrels per day, in 2030 it will be 118 million barrels per day. Experts say that wind power will not be able to fill this demand.

Paving Nature to Harness Wind

Wind turbines cannot be lined up in a row as the resulting turbulence would lower the downwind turbines to zero production if not destroy them from asymmetrical wind forces. So there is just so much power that can be generated per acre of wind farm. And remember, these will have to be sited in areas that some *environmentalists* will go to the wall for to prevent development, including the construction of transmission lines.

The figure given by the EPA [Environmental Protection Agency], assuming a 30-percent capacity factor, is 1.23 watts per square meter, or about 5 kW per acre. At our lower capacity factor, this becomes roughly 2.5 kW per acre so that over a year's time there would 21,900 kWh per acre of electrical generation.

Returning to our 6.9 billion kWh required by the politicians, we see that the wind farms would require 316,400 acres to meet their demands—a mere 494 square miles. Well, there goes The Natural State.

Coal Plants Could Not Be Replaced

But at least we could get rid of some of our polluting coal power plants, right? Well actually, no we couldn't. The weather in the United States is often dominated in both summer and winter by what is known as a "dome of high pressure." Such a condition leads to winds that are "light and variable"—certainly not of a quality to turn a wind turbine. Consequently, all the existing power plants would have to remain.

How can I possibly claim that every kilowatt hour generated by wind power doesn't eliminate that much pollution from a coal-fired plant? Because it's true. Most of our country is tied together in an electrical grid so that power can be routed from one area to another as demands change from place to place. Electricity is not stored on the grid. If a portion of the power comes from wind generation, there must always be a backup in the event this drops significantly—like perhaps to zero. These backup plants must be kept running as it requires hours if not days to bring them up to a level where they can provide power.

Noisy Bird Killers

Wind power enthusiasts become very defensive when reminded that wind turbines produce annoying noise and kill large numbers of birds. Wind-power promoters point out that good aerodynamic design and the noise produced naturally by the wind masks the "whooshing" sound of the turbines that some people consider objectionable. But

Some claim that wind cannot provide a constant supply of energy in sufficient quantities to replace oil.

there's more to turbine noise than a mere "whooshing" sound. Left unaddressed is the low frequency thumping noise caused as each blade passes the supporting structure. In rural areas, particularly at night when ambient noise levels are low, the thumping interrupts sleep and leads to related health issues. This noise has led the French Academy of Medicine to call for a halt of turbine projects within 1.5 kilometers (0.9 miles) of any residence. Similarly, the U.K. Noise Association recommends a one-mile setback from residential areas.

As for birds killed by turbines, it has been noted that an unusual number of raptors—hawks, owls, eagles—along with bats fall victim to the 200-mile-per-hour turbine blades. One theory behind the significant numbers of raptors killed, as opposed to other birds—say songbirds—is that birds of prey have eyes oriented in a forward direction, while other birds (the preyed upon) have eyes on the sides of their heads and are able to detect the motion of the blades more readily. Whatever the reason for the deaths, it has caused the U.S. Fish and Wildlife Service to issue siting guidelines recommending that wind turbines not be installed near wetlands, mountain ridges, or shorelines where birds tend to concentrate.

Wind Power Is Too Costly

If wind power is so unreliable, doesn't replace power plants, and promises to have many siting restrictions, why would anyone support it? Perhaps the most reliable method of analyzing a government project is the old standby: follow the money trail. While no estimates have surfaced regarding the costs of this project nationally, we can look at Arkansas as representative of the country and use it to determine how much money will be spent to meet the needs of this junk science. You may recall that Arkansas, which represents about one percent of the energy equation, requires 3,516 1.5-megawatt turbines to produce the required capacity for that state's "renewable" energy. The average cost of wind turbine generators is about $1.5 million per megawatt. Catch your breath and do the math: $7.9 billion. And that's just Arkansas! Nationwide the taxpayers would need to cough up $790 billion to implement this scheme. In 1991, the Interstate Highway System was considered complete at a cost of $129 billion. Taking into account inflation since 1991, the proposed cost of wind power would be over 4 times the cost of the interstates.

Kept Alive by Government Subsidies

You may wonder, "If wind turbines aren't useful as a source of power, why were so many being built even before the House passed its legislation?" The answer is government subsidies.

A case study of how wind power is dependent on government subsidies and dictates is the Cape Wind project, a proposed wind-turbine complex slated to be built offshore from Cape Cod in Nantucket Sound. That project became notorious because of opposition from ultraliberal U.S. Senator Edward Kennedy, who was not concerned about the cost but didn't want the view from his yacht infringed upon. David G. Tuerck, executive director of the Beacon Hill Institute, analyzed the pro forma information on the project and noted: "What we found was quite remarkable. Cape Wind stands to receive subsidies worth $731 million, or 77 percent of the cost of installing the project and 48 percent of the revenues it would generate." This project was given final approval by the State of Massachusetts last March, and is now awaiting other government approvals.

Without government interference in the marketplace, wind power would be a relic for our historical entertainment. Do U.S. congressmen have any idea of the physical realities of what they have just voted for or its costs or consequences? Obviously not. Guess it's time we told them.

EVALUATING THE AUTHORS' ARGUMENTS:

Hiserodt describes wind power as an environmentally unfriendly power source. Name at least two ways in which wind power could hurt the environment, according to Hiserodt. How do you think Mark Lambrides and Juan Cruz Monticelli, authors of the previous viewpoint, would respond to these charges? After analyzing both authors' claims, state your opinion on whether wind power is an environmentally friendly power source, using evidence from the text to back up your points.

Oil Should Be Replaced with Biofuels

"The more one can fiddle with the ethanol-producing microbes to reduce the number of steps in the conversion process, the lower costs will be, and the sooner cellulosic ethanol will become commercially competitive."

Jamie Shreeve

In the following viewpoint experts describe different approaches to using genetically modified organisms to produce ethanol cheaply and efficiently enough to replace oil. They claim that the raw materials for biofuel production are "nearly unlimited" due to the ability to use biomass sources like agricultural waste.

Jamie [James] Shreeve is the author of *The Genome War: How Craig Venter Tried to Capture the Code of Life and Save the World, The Neanderthal Enigma: Solving the Mystery of Modern Human Origins*, and coauthor of *Lucy's Child: The Discovery of a Human Ancestor*. His articles have appeared in publications including *National Geographic, Discover*, and *Smithsonian*.

AS YOU READ, CONSIDER THE FOLLOWING QUESTIONS:

1. What event originally triggered an increase in ethanol production?
2. According to Greg Stephanopoulos, why isn't it simple to engineer an organism that makes ethanol?
3. What energy sources besides ethanol can microbes produce?

P roducing ethanol fuel from biomass is attractive for a number of reasons. At a time of soaring gas prices and worries over the long-term availability of foreign oil, the domestic supply of raw materials for making biofuels appears nearly unlimited. Meanwhile, the amount of carbon dioxide dumped into the atmosphere annually by burning fossil fuels is projected to rise worldwide from about 24 billion metric tons in 2002 to 33 billion metric tons in 2015. Burning a gallon of ethanol, on the other hand, adds little to the total carbon in the atmosphere, since the carbon dioxide given off in the process is roughly equal to the amount absorbed by the plants used to produce the next gallon.

Using ethanol for auto fuel is hardly a new idea. . . . Since the energy crisis of the early 1970s, tax incentives have pushed ethanol production up; in 2005, it reached four billion gallons a year. But that still translates to only 3 percent of the fuel in American gas tanks. One reason for the limited use of ethanol is that in the United States, it's made almost exclusively from cornstarch; the process is inefficient and competes with other agricultural uses of corn. While it is relatively easy to convert the starch in corn kernels into the sugars needed to produce ethanol, the fuel yield is low compared with the amount of energy that goes into raising and harvesting the crops. Processing ethanol from cellulose–wheat and rice straw, switchgrass, paper pulp, agricultural waste products like corn cobs and leaves–has the potential to squeeze at least twice as much fuel from the same area of land, because so much more biomass is available per acre. Moreover, such an approach would use feedstocks that are otherwise essentially worthless.

FAST FACT

Biofuels are made from corn, sugar, tapioca, wood, trees, switchgrass, sorghum, and soybean, coconut, palm, canola, and jatropha nut oil. These fuels come mostly from Brazil (38 percent of the world's supply), the United States (24 percent), and the European Union (12 percent).

Genetic Engineering Can Increase Ethanol Production

Converting cellulose to ethanol involves two fundamental steps: breaking the long chains of cellulose molecules into glucose and other sugars,

High school students in Vermont present their plan to use switchgrass-based pellets as biofuel to the state's Senate Agriculture Committee.

and fermenting those sugars into ethanol. In nature, these processes are performed by different organisms: fungi and bacteria that use enzymes (cellulases) to "free" the sugar in cellulose, and other microbes, primarily yeasts, that ferment sugars into alcohol. . . . The more one can fiddle with the ethanol-producing microbes to reduce the number of steps in the conversion process, the lower costs will be, and the sooner cellulosic ethanol will become commercially competitive. In conventional production, for instance, ethanol has to be continually removed from fermentation reactors, because the yeasts cannot tolerate too much of it. MIT's Greg Stephanopoulos, a professor of chemical engineering, has developed a yeast that can tolerate 50 percent more ethanol. But, he says, such genetic engineering involves more than just splicing in a gene or two. "The question isn't whether we can make an organism that makes ethanol," says Stephanopoulos. "It's how we can engineer a whole network of reactions to convert different sugars into ethanol at high yields and productivities. Ethanol tolerance is a property of the system, not a single gene. If we want to increase the overall yield, we have to manipulate many genes at the same time."

The ideal organism would do it all–break down cellulose like a bacterium, ferment sugar like a yeast, tolerate high concentrations of ethanol, and devote most of its metabolic resources to producing just ethanol. There are two strategies for creating such an all-purpose bug. One is to modify an existing microbe by adding desired genetic pathways from other organisms and "knocking out" undesirable ones; the other is to start with the clean slate of a stripped-down synthetic cell and build a custom genome almost from scratch.

Shortening Ethanol Production to One Step

Lee Lynd, an engineering professor at Dartmouth University, is betting on the first approach. He and his colleagues want to collapse the many biologically mediated steps involved in ethanol production into one. "This is a potentially game-changing breakthrough in low-cost processing of cellulosic biomass," he says. The strategy could involve either modifying an organism that naturally metabolizes cellulose so that it produces high yields of ethanol, or engineering a natural ethanol producer so that it metabolizes cellulose.

This May, Lynd and his colleagues reported advances on both fronts. A team from the University of Stellenbosch in South Africa that had collaborated with Lynd announced that it had designed a yeast that can survive on cellulose alone, breaking down the complex molecules and fermenting the resultant simple sugars into ethanol. At the same time, Lynd's group reported engineering a "thermophilic" bacterium–one that naturally lives in high-temperature environments–whose only fermentation product is ethanol. Other organisms have been engineered to perform similar sleights of hand at normal temperatures, but Lynd's recombinant microbe does so at the high temperatures where commercial cellulases work best. "We're much closer to commercial use than people think," says Lynd, who is commercializing advanced ethanol technology at Mascoma, a startup in Cambridge, MA.

Engineering Microbes to Make Gasoline

Others are pursuing a far more radical approach. . . . Synthetic Genomics is in hot pursuit of a bacterium "that will do everything," as [Craig] Venter puts it. With funding from Synthetic Genomics, scientists at the J. Craig Venter Institute are adding and subtracting

How Ethanol Is Made

Ethanol for fuel is made by the same process that produces moonshine. Grain is crushed, fermented for several days, and distilled to remove water.

1. Corn kernels are removed.

2. Kernels are then crushed in a mill.

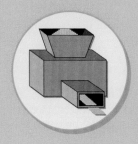

3. Water and enzymes are added to the corn in a fermenter. Yeast is added later.

4. Alcohol-containing "beer" is pumped into boiler and heated.

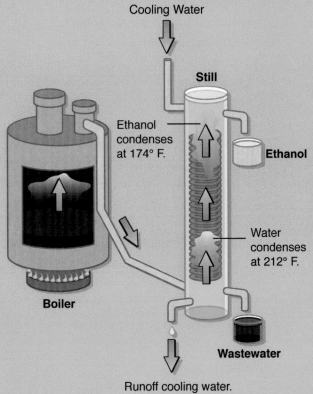

Cooling Water

Still

Ethanol condenses at 174° F.

Ethanol

Water condenses at 212° F.

Boiler

Wastewater

Runoff cooling water.

5. Ethanol has been created.

Taken from: Mike Allen, "Crunching the Numbers on Alternative Fuels," *Popular Mechanics*, May 2006.

genes from natural organisms using the recombinant techniques employed by other microbial engineers. . . . Among biofuels, ethanol is the established front-runner, but various types of microbes also produce hydrogen, methane, biodiesel, and even electricity—which means they could be genetically engineered to produce more of these resources. At the University of California, Berkeley, bioengineer Jay Keasling and his colleagues are proposing to design organisms that pump out a fuel no natural microbe makes, one that offers some alluring advantages over ethanol: gasoline. Its virtues as a fuel are proven, of course, and the ability to produce it from waste wood and waste paper, which Keasling thinks is feasible, could reduce countries' dependence on foreign oil. And unlike ethanol, which is water soluble and must be transported in trucks lest it pick up water in pipes, biologically generated octane could be economically piped to consumers, just like today's gas. . . . In the short term, some advances in biology and engineering are needed before fuels made from biomass will be practical and competitive with fossil fuels. But in the longer term, says Venter, "we're limited mostly by our imagination, not by the limits of biology."

EVALUATING THE AUTHOR'S ARGUMENTS:

In this viewpoint Shreeve presents different ways in which ethanol can be produced that involve modifying the genes of various organisms. What are they? In your opinion which method seems like it will be most successful?

Oil Should Not Be Replaced with Biofuels

Brian Tokar

"The ethanol gold rush [is] nothing more than the subsidized burning of food to run automobiles."

In the following viewpoint Brian Tokar argues that biofuels cannot reduce America's oil consumption. Citing two prominent studies, Tokar argues that in most cases, it takes more energy to turn biomatter into a fuel than the biofuel can provide. The amount of energy used to produce biofuels, therefore, negates any real energy gains in the finished product—especially in contrast to gasoline. The author further argues that the amount of land required to produce these biofuels—namely corn, soy, and sugarcane—would take away land used for food crops and would put enormous pressure on the world's water resources. For these reasons, Tokar concludes that biofuels are unable to provide a long-term solution to the planet's energy needs.

Tokar is the director of the Biotechnology Project at Vermont's Institute for Social Ecology. He has edited two books about genetic engineering—*Redesigning Life?* and *Gene Traders: Biotechnology, World Trade and the Globalization of Hunger.*

Brian Tokar, "The Real Scoop on Biofuels: 'Green Energy' Panacea or Just the Latest Hype?" *WW4 Report*, ww4report.com/node/2864, November 1, 2006. Reproduced by permission of the author.

AS YOU READ, CONSIDER THE FOLLOWING QUESTIONS:
1. According to Tokar the amount of grain required to fill the tank of an SUV could have what other purpose?
2. How much energy does it take to turn switchgrass, wood, and sunflowers into fuel, according to the author?
3. What is a major source of Brazil's greenhouse gas emissions, as reported by the author?

Y ou can hardly open up a major newspaper or national magazine these days without encountering the latest hype about biofuels, and how they're going to save oil, reduce pollution and prevent climate change. Bill Gates, Sun Microsystems' Vinod Khosla, and other major venture capitalists are investing millions in new biofuel production, whether in the form of ethanol, mainly derived from corn in the US today, or biodiesel, mainly from soybeans and canola seed. It's literally a "modern day gold rush," as described by the *New York Times*, paraphrasing the chief executive of Cargill, one of the main benefactors of increased subsidies to agribusiness and tax credits to refiners for the purpose of encouraging biofuel production. . . .

Burning Food to Run Autos

Several well-respected analysts have raised serious concerns about this rapid diversion of food crops toward the production of fuel for automobiles. WorldWatch Institute founder Lester Brown, long concerned about the sustainability of world food supplies, says that fuel producers are already competing—with food processors in the world's grain markets. "Cars, not people, will claim most of the increase in grain production this year," reports Brown—a serious concern in a world where the grain required to make enough ethanol to fill an SUV tank is enough to feed a person for a whole year. Others have dismissed the ethanol gold rush as nothing more than the subsidized burning of food to run automobiles.

The biofuel rush is having a significant impact worldwide as well. Brazil, often touted as the the most impressive biofuel success story, is using half its annual sugarcane crop to provide 40% of its auto fuel, while accelerating deforestation to grow more sugarcane and soybeans.

Malaysian and Indonesian rainforests are being bulldozed for oil palm plantations—threatening endangered orangutans, rhinos, tigers and countless other species—in order to serve at the booming European market for biodiesel.

Biofuel Production Will Harm the Environment

Are these reasonable tradeoffs for a troubled planet, or merely another corporate push for profits? Two recent studies aim to document the full consequences of the new biofuel economy and realistically assess its impact on fuel use, greenhouse gases and agricultural lands. One study, originating from the University of Minnesota, is moderately hopeful in the first two areas, but offers a strong caution about land use. The other, from Cornell University and UC Berkeley, concludes that every domestic biofuel source—those currently in use as well as those under development—produce less energy than is consumed in growing and processing the crops.

The Minnesota researchers attempted a full lifecycle analysis of the production of ethanol from corn and biodiesel from soy. They documented the energy costs of fuel production, pesticide use, transportation, and other key factors, and also accounted for the energy equivalent of soy and corn byproducts that remain for other uses after the fuel is extracted. Their paper, published in the July 25, 2006 edition of the *Proceedings of the National Academy of Sciences*, concluded that ethanol production offers a modest net energy gain of 25% over oil, resulting in 12% less greenhouse gases than an equivalent amount of gasoline. The numbers for biodiesel are more promising, with a 93% net energy gain and a 41% reduction in greenhouse gases.

> ## FAST FACT
>
> According to biofuels expert David Pimentel, professor of ecology and agriculture at Cornell University, biofuels have a negative net energy, meaning more energy is needed to make them than they offer as fuel. For example, it takes 6,597 kilocalories of fossil fuel energy to make a liter of ethanol, which contains only 5,130 kilocalories of viable fuel—a 22 percent net loss.

It Takes Fossil Energy to Make Biofuel

Biofuels may burn clean and be renewable, but they cannot be made without fossil fuel. Because the process of making biofuel uses so much fossil energy, they have what is called a negative net energy—meaning that it takes more energy to make them than they provide when burned.

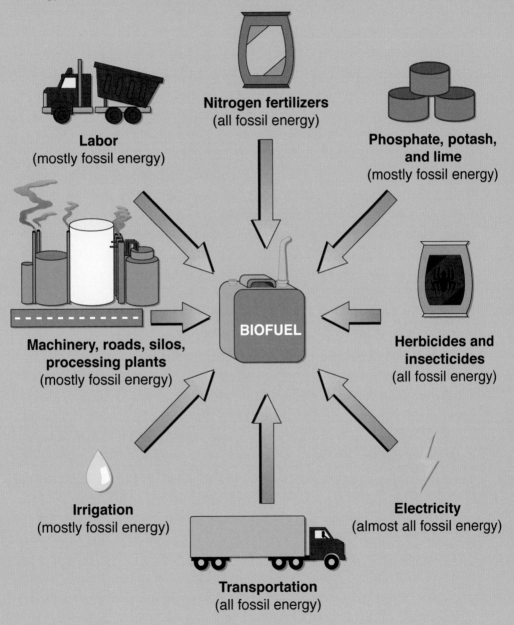

Nitrogen fertilizers
(all fossil energy)

Labor
(mostly fossil energy)

Phosphate, potash, and lime
(mostly fossil energy)

Machinery, roads, silos, processing plants
(mostly fossil energy)

BIOFUEL

Herbicides and insecticides
(all fossil energy)

Irrigation
(mostly fossil energy)

Transportation
(all fossil energy)

Electricity
(almost all fossil energy)

The researchers cautioned, however, that these figures do not account for the significant environmental damage from increased acreages of these crops, including the impacts of pesticides, nitrate runoff into water supplies, nor the increased demand on water, as "energy crops" like corn and soy begin to displace more drought tolerant crops such as wheat in several Midwestern states.

A Serious Strain on Land

The most serious impact, though, is on land use. The Minnesota paper reports that in 2005, 14% of the US corn harvest was used to produce some 3.9 billion gallons of ethanol, equivalent to 1.7% of current gasoline usage. About 1 1/2 percent of the soy harvest produced 68 million gallons of biodiesel, equivalent to less than one tenth of one percent of gas usage. This means that if all of the country's corn harvest was used to make ethanol, it would displace 12% of our gas; all of our soybeans would displace about 6% of diesel use. But if the energy used in producing these biofuels is taken into account, the picture becomes worse still. It requires roughly eight units of gas to produce 10 units of ethanol, and five units of gas to produce 10 units of biodiesel; hence the net is only two units of ethanol or five units of biodiesel. Therefore the entire soy and corn crops combined would really only less than 3% of current gasoline and diesel use. This is where the serious strain on food supplies and prices originates.

The Cornell study is even more skeptical. Released in July 2005, it was the product of an ongoing collaboration between Cornell agriculturalist David Pimentel, environmental engineer Ted Patzek, and their colleagues at the University of California at Berkeley, and was published in the journal *Natural Resources Research*. This study found that, on balance, making ethanol from corn requires 29% more fossil fuel than the net energy produced and biodiesel from soy results in a net energy loss of 27%. Other crops, touted as solutions to the apparent diseconomy of current methods, offer even worse results.

Switchgrass, for example, can grow on marginal land and presumably won't compete with food production (you may recall George Bush's mumbling about switchgrass in his 2006 State of the Union speech), but it requires 45% more energy to harvest and process than the energy value of the fuel that is produced. Wood biomass requires

57% more energy than it produces, and sunflowers require more than twice as much energy than is available in the fuel that is produced. "There is just no energy benefit to using plant biomass for liquid fuel," said David Pimentel in a Cornell press statement this past July. "These strategies are not sustainable." In a recent article, Harvard environmental scientist Michael McElroy concurred: "[U]nfortunately the promised benefits [of ethanol] prove upon analysis to be largely ephemeral."

Biofuels Encourage Deforestation

Even Brazilian sugarcane, touted as the world's model for conversion from fossil fuels to sustainable "green energy," has its downside. The energy yield appears beyond question: it is claimed that ethanol from sugarcane may produce as much as 8 times as much energy as it takes

Some people are concerned that biofuels will divert resources from growing food crops and that it could actually increase global climate change.

to grow and process. But a recent World Wildlife Fund report for the International Energy Agency raises serious questions about this approach to future energy independence. It turns out that 80% of Brazil's greenhouse gas emissions come not from cars, but from deforestation—the loss of embedded carbon dioxide when forests are cut down and burned. A hectare of land may save 13 tons of carbon dioxide if it is used to grow sugarcane, but the same hectare can absorb 20 tons of CO_2 if it remains forested. If sugarcane and soy plantations continue to encourage deforestation, both in the Amazon and in Brazil's Atlantic coastal forests, any climate advantage is more than outweighed by the loss of the forest. . . .

Biofuels Are Not a Long-Term Solution

Biofuels may still prove advantageous in some local applications, such as farmers using crop wastes to fuel their farms, and running cars from waste oil that is otherwise thrown away by restaurants. But as a solution to long-term energy needs on a national or international scale, the costs appear to far outweigh the benefits.

EVALUATING THE AUTHORS' ARGUMENTS:

Brian Tokar states that switchgrass is not a productive and effective biofuel because it requires 45 percent more energy to produce and harvest than the energy value of the plant itself. In the preceding article Jamie Shreeve argues that switchgrass and other forms of cellulose can be a plentiful source of biofuel. With which author do you agree? Does one author provide better evidence than the other? Explain your answer thoroughly.

Oil Use in the United States

According to the U.S. Energy Information Administration, energy used in the United States comes from oil and several other sources:

- Crude oil and petroleum account for 40 percent of America's energy needs;
- coal, 23 percent;
- natural gas, 23 percent;
- nuclear power, 8 percent; and
- renewable resources, 6 percent.

According to the Energy Information Administration:

- The United States uses about 20.8 million barrels of oil every day.
- Fossil fuels account for nearly 80 percent of America's energy.
- It takes the equivalent of 7 gallons of gasoline per day for every man, woman, and child to keep the United States running at its current pace.
- The United States is home to 4 percent of the world's population, yet consumes 26 percent of the world's energy.
- U.S. demand is projected to increase to 27 million barrels of oil per day by 2020. Sixty-four percent of this will need to be imported.

Oil Use Around the World

The top petroleum-consuming countries as of 2007 were:

1. United States (26 percent of the total oil consumed every day)
2. Japan (7 percent)
3. China (6 percent)
4. Germany (3.6 percent)
5. Russia (3.3 percent)
6. Brazil (2.8 percent)
7. South Korea (2.8 percent)
8. Canada (2.7 percent)
9. France (2.6 percent)
10. India (2.6 percent)
11. Mexico (2.6 percent)

12. Italy (2.4 percent)
13. United Kingdom (2.2 percent)
14. Spain (1.9 percent)
15. Saudi Arabia (1.7 percent)
16. Iran (1.4 percent)
17. Indonesia (1.3 percent)
18. Australia (1.1 percent)
19. The Netherlands (1.1 percent)
20. Taiwan (1.1 percent)
21. rest of the world (23 percent)

According to the Energy Information Administration:
- Current global consumption of oil is about 86 million barrels of oil per day. That equals 3.1 billion gallons of oil every day.
- Global oil consumption is projected to rise to 100 million barrels per day by the year 2016.
- World oil demand is projected to increase to 118.9 million barrels per day in 2020.
- By 2025 global oil consumption is expected to be between 117 and 125 millions of barrels per day.
- The 1 billion people in the industrialized world now consume 60 percent of world oil production, or an average of 18 barrels per person each year.
- The 5 billion people in developing countries, such as China and India, consume 33 million barrels per day, or 2.4 barrels per person each year.

According to Shell Oil, if the world continues to consume oil at the current rate, the world supply will last another forty-two years.

According to the Environmental Defense Fund, in 2004 American cars produced 314 million metric tons of carbon dioxide (CO_2)—about the amount of carbon in a coal train fifty-five thousand miles long, and enough to circle the world twice.

According to the British Broadcasting Company:
- The world's largest known oil reserves are in the Middle East: Saudi Arabia, Iraq, the United Arab Emirates, Kuwait, and Iran.
- Each American burns 25 barrels of oil a year; each Briton burns 11; each Chinese burns 2.

- Fewer and fewer major new oil fields are discovered each year:
    16 were discovered in 2000
    9 were discovered in 2001
    1 was discovered in 2005
- Products made from petroleum include: DVDs, perfume, food preservatives, detergents, plastics, deodorants, medicines, explosives, carpets, contact lenses, paint, crayons, ink, bubble gum, dish washing liquids, eyeglasses, records, tires, ammonia, and heart valves.
- Oil provides about 40 percent of the energy Americans consume and 97 percent of U.S. transportation fuels.

Supply

As of January 1, 2006, proven oil reserves amounted to about 1,293 billion barrels. One barrel equals 42 gallons, or 159 liters. The countries with the largest reserves are:

- Saudi Arabia (264.3 billion barrels)
- Canada (178.8 billion barrels)
- Iran (132.5 billion barrels)
- Iraq (115 billion barrels)
- Kuwait (101.5 billion barrels)
- United Arab Emirates (97.8 billion barrels)
- Venezuela (79.7 billion barrels)
- Russia (60.0 billion barrels)
- Libya (39.1 billion barrels)
- Nigeria (35.9 billion barrels)
- United States (21.4 billion barrels)
- China (18.3 billion barrels)
- Qatar (15.2 billion barrels)
- Mexico (12.9 billion barrels)
- Algeria (11.4 billion barrels)
- Brazil (11.2 billion barrels)
- Kazakhstan (9.0 billion barrels)
- Norway (7.7 billion barrels)
- Azerbaijan (7.0 billion barrels)
- India (5.8 billion barrels)
- rest of the world (68.1 billion barrels)

Of the world's total proven oil reserves, 71 percent are located in the Middle East or Canada.

The top petroleum-producing states in the United States are:
1. Texas
2. Alaska
3. California
4. Louisiana
5. New Mexico

As of 2006 the nations that supplied the most crude oil to the United States were:

1. Canada (1,797 barrels per day)
2. Mexico (1,469 barrels per day)
3. Saudi Arabia (1,434 barrels per day)
4. Venezuela (1,167 barrels per day)
5. Nigeria (890 barrels per day)
6. Algeria (520 barrels per day)
7. Iraq (460 barrels per day)
8. Angola (392 barrels per day)
9. Colombia (207 barrels per day)
10. Kuwait (197 barrels per day)
11. Libya (165 barrels per day)
12. United Kingdom (162 barrels per day)
13. Ecuador (159 barrels per day)
14. Brazil (147 barrels per day)
15. Equatorial Guinea (113 barrels per day)

Organizations to Contact

The editors have compiled the following list of organizations concerned with the issues debated in this book. The descriptions are derived from materials provided by the organizations. All have publications or information available for interested readers. The list was compiled on the date of publication of the present volume; names, addresses, and phone numbers may change. Be aware that many organizations take several weeks or longer to respond to inquiries, so allow as much time as possible.

American Petroleum Institute (API)
1220 L St. NW
Washington, DC 20005
(202) 682-8000
www.api.org

The American Petroleum Institute is a trade association representing America's petroleum industry. Its activities include lobbying, conducting research, and setting technical standards for the petroleum industry. API publishes numerous position papers, reports, and information sheets.

American Solar Energy Society (ASES)
2400 Central Ave., Suite G-1
Boulder, CO 80301
(303) 443-3130
fax: (303) 443-3212
e-mail: ases@ases.org
www.ases.org

ASES promotes solar energy. It disseminates information on solar energy to schools, universities, and the community. In addition to the *ASES Publications Catalog*, the society publishes the bimonthly magazine *Solar Today*.

American Wind Energy Association (AWEA)
122 C St. NW, Suite 380
Washington, DC 20001

(202) 383-2500
fax: (202) 383-2505
e-mail: windmail@awea.org
www.awea.org

The American Wind Energy Association is a national trade association that represents wind power plant developers, wind turbine manufacturers, utilities, consultants, insurers, financiers, researchers, and others involved in the wind industry. The AWEA promotes wind energy as a clean source of electricity for consumers around the world. The association provides statistics and information on development in the domestic and international markets to industry interests, the general public, and the news media. Publications include industry documents, the latest economic studies, technology information, and books.

Cato Institute
1000 Massachusetts Ave. NW
Washington, DC 20001-5403
(202) 842-0200
fax: (202) 842-3490
e-mail: cato@cato.org
www.cato.org

The Cato Institute is a libertarian public policy research foundation that aims to limit the role of government and protect civil liberties. The institute believes EPA regulations are too stringent. Publications offered on the Web site include the bimonthly *Cato Policy Report*, the quarterly journal *Regulation*, and numerous papers that deal with energy policy.

Committee for a Constructive Tomorrow (CFACT)
PO Box 65722
Washington, DC 20035
(202) 429-2737
e-mail: info@cfact.org
www.cfact.org

The Committee for a Constructive Tomorrow supports continued development of technologies such as agricultural chemicals, atomic power, and biotechnology. CFACT works to promote free market and technological solutions to such growing concerns as energy production. The committee produces a national radio commentary called *Just the Facts* that is heard daily on about three hundred stations across the country.

Competitive Enterprise Institute (CEI)
1001 Connecticut Ave. NW, Suite 1250
Washington, DC 20036
(202) 331-1010
fax: (202) 331-0640
e-mail: info@cei.org
www.cei.org

CEI is a nonprofit public policy organization dedicated to the principles of free enterprise and limited government. The institute believes private incentives and property rights, rather than government regulations, are the best way to protect the environment. CEI's publications include the newsletter *Monthly Planet, OnPoint* policy briefs, and the books *Global Warming and Other Eco-Myths* and *The True State of the Planet.*

Council on Alternative Fuels (CAF)
1225 I St. NW, Suite 320
Washington, DC 20005
(202) 898-0711

CAF is comprised of companies interested in the production of synthetic fuels and the research and development of synthetic fuel technology. It publishes information on new alternative fuels in the monthly publication *Alternate Fuel News.*

Ecological Life Systems Institute (ELSI)
PO Box 7453
San Diego, CA 92167
(619) 758-9020
fax: (619) 758-9029
e-mail: info@elsi.org
www.elsi.org

The goals of the Ecological Life Systems Institute include learning how people can earn a living in ways that are economically sustainable. To do so, the ELSI identifies and promotes policies and practices that advises the health of the environment and teaches that knowledge to others in classrooms, industry, and government. The institute's Web site has dozens of articles concerning oil, renewable energy, global warming, and related topics.

Energy Conservation Coalition (ECC)
1525 New Hampshire Ave. NW
Washington, DC 20036
(202) 745-4874

ECC is a group of public interest organizations that promotes energy sufficiency. It supports government policies that encourage energy conservation. ECC publishes *Powerline*, a bimonthly periodical covering consumer issues on energy and utilities.

Environmental Protection Agency (EPA)
Ariel Rios Building, 1200 Pennsylvania Ave. NW
Washington, DC 20460
(202) 272-0167
www.epa.gov

The EPA is the federal agency in charge of protecting the environment and controlling pollution. The agency works toward these goals by enacting and enforcing regulations, identifying and fining polluters, assisting businesses and local environmental agencies, and cleaning up polluted sites. The EPA publishes periodic reports and the monthly *EPA Activities Update*.

Foundation for Clean Air Progress (FCAP)
1801 K St. NW, Suite 1000L
Washington, DC 20036
(800) 272-1604
e-mail: info@cleanairprogress.org
www.cleanairprogress.org

FCAP is a nonprofit organization that believes the public is unaware of the progress that has been made in reducing air pollution. The foundation represents various sectors of business and industry in providing information to the public about improving air quality trends. FCAP publishes reports and studies demonstrating that air pollution is on the decline, including *Breathing Easier About Energy—A Healthy Economy* and *Healthier Air and Study on Air Quality Trends, 1970–2015*.

Friends on Earth
1025 Vermont Ave. NW, Suite 300
Washington, DC 20005
(202) 783-7400

Friends of the Earth is dedicated to protecting the planet from environmental disaster and to preserving biological diversity. The organization encourages energy policies that are environmentally and socially responsible. Its publications include the bimonthly newsletter *Friends of the Earth* and the book *Crude Awakening, the Oil Mess in America: Wasting Energy, Jobs, and the Environment.*

Global Warming International Center (GWIC)
22W381 75th St.
Naperville, IL 60565
(630) 910-1551
fax: (630) 910-1561
www.globalwarming.net

GWIC is an international body that provides information on global warming science and policy to industries and governmental and nongovernmental organizations. The center sponsors research supporting the understanding of global warming and ways to reduce the problem. It publishes the quarterly newsletter *World Resource Review.*

International Association for Hydrogen Energy (IAHE)
5783 SW 40 St., #303
Miami, FL 33155
(305) 284-4666
www.iahe.org

The IAHE is a group of scientists and engineers professionally involved with the production and use of hydrogen. It sponsors international forums to further its goal of creating an energy system based on hydrogen. The IAHE publishes the monthly *International Journal for Hydrogen Energy.*

National Biodiesel Board (NBB)
3337A Emerald Ln., PO Box 104898
Jefferson City, MO 65110
(573) 635-3893
fax: (573) 635-7913
e-mail: info@biodiesel.org
www.biodiesel.org

The National Biodiesel Board is a national trade association representing the biodiesel industry and acts as the coordinating body for biodiesel research and development in the United States. It was founded in 1992 by state soybean commodity groups, who were funding biodiesel research and development programs. Since that time, NBB's membership has included state, national, and international feedstock and feedstock processor organizations, biodiesel suppliers, fuel marketers and distributors, and technology providers. In addition to distributing books and brochures concerning biodiesel, the NBB publishes the *Biodiesel Bulletin*, a monthly newsletter.

The National Renewable Energy Laboratory (NREL)
1617 Cole Blvd.
Golden, CO 80401-3393
(303) 275-3000
www.nrel.gov

The National Renewable Energy Laboratory is the U.S. Department of Energy's laboratory for renewable energy research, development, and deployment, and a leading laboratory for energy efficiency. The laboratory's mission is to develop renewable energy and energy efficiency technologies and practices, advance related science and engineering, and transfer knowledge and innovations to address the nation's energy and environmental goals. Some of the areas of scientific investigation at NREL include wind energy, biomass-derived fuels, advanced vehicles, solar manufacturing, hydrogen fuel cells, and waste-to-energy technologies. The organization publishes dozens of comprehensive research papers concerning these technologies, many of them available for free online.

Natural Resources Defense Council (NRDC)
40 W. 20th St.
New York, NY 10011
(212) 727-2700
fax: (212) 727-1773
e-mail: nrdcinfo@nrdc.org
www.nrdc.org

The NRDC is a nonprofit organization with more than four hundred thousand members. It uses laws and science to protect the environment. NRDC publishes the quarterly magazine *OnEarth* and hundreds of reports concerned with oil and energy policy.

Nuclear Energy Institute (NEI)
1776 I St. NW, Suite 400
Washington, DC 20006-3708

(202) 739-8000
fax: (202) 785-4019
e-mail: webmasterp@nei.org
www.nei.org

The Nuclear Energy Institute is the policy organization of the nuclear energy industry whose objective is to promote policies that benefit the nuclear energy business. NEI develops policy on key legislative and regulatory issues affecting the nuclear industry. The organization has over 260 corporate members in fifteen countries, including companies that operate nuclear power plants, design and engineering firms, fuel suppliers and service companies, and companies involved in nuclear medicine and nuclear industrial applications. NEI publishes numerous books and brochures that promote nuclear energy and safety.

Pew Center on Global Climate Change
2101 Wilson Blvd., Suite 550
Arlington, VA 22201
(703) 516-4146
fax: (703) 841-1422
www.pewclimate.org

The Pew Center is a nonpartisan organization dedicated to educating the public and policy makers about the causes and potential consequences of global climate change and informing them of ways to reduce the emissions of greenhouse gases. Its reports include *Designing a Climate-Friendly Energy Policy* and *The Science of Climate Change.*

Political Economy Research Center (PERC)
2048 Analysis Dr., Suite A
Bozeman, MT 59718
(406) 587-9591
e-mail: perc@perc.org
www.perc.org

PERC is a nonprofit research and educational organization that seeks market-oriented solutions to environmental problems. The center holds a variety of conferences and provides environmental educational material. Many of its publications focus on the problem of how to meet the world's energy needs in a sustainable and environmental way.

Reason Foundation
3415 S. Sepulveda Blvd., Suite 400
Los Angeles, CA 90034-6064

(310) 391-2245
fax: (310) 391-4395

The Reason Foundation is a libertarian public policy research organization. Its environmental research focuses on issues such as energy, global warming, and recycling. The foundation publishes the monthly magazine *Reason* and the books *Global Warming: The Greenhouse, White House, and Poor House Effect, The Case Against Electric Vehicle Mandates in California,* and *Solid Waste Recycling Costs—Issues and Answers.*

Renewable Energy Policy Project (REPP)
1612 K St NW, Suite 202
Washington, DC 20006
(202) 293-2898
fax: (202) 298-5857
e-mail: info2@repp.org
www.repp.org

Renewable Energy Policy Project provides information about solar, hydrogen, biomass, wind, and other forms of "green" energy. The goal of the group is to accelerate the use of renewable energy by providing credible facts, policy analysis, and innovative strategies concerning renewables. REPP seeks to define growth strategies for renewables that respond to competitive energy markets and environmental needs. The project has a comprehensive online library of publications dedicated to these issues.

Renewable Fuels Association (RFA)
1 Massachusetts Ave. NW, Suite 820
Washington, DC 20001
(202) 289-3935
fax: (202) 289-7519
e-mail: info@ethanolrfa.org
www.ethanolrfa.org

RFA is comprised of professionals who research, produce, and market renewable fuels, especially alcohol fuels. It also represents the renewable fuels industry before the federal government. RFA publishes the monthly newsletter *Ethanol Report.*

Union of Concerned Scientists (UCS)
2 Brattle Square
Cambridge, MA 02238

(617) 547-5552
fax: (617) 864-9405
e-mail: ucs@ucsusa.org
www.ucsusa.org

UCS aims to advance responsible public policy in areas where science and technology play important roles. Its programs emphasize transportation reform, arms control, safe and renewable energy technologies, and sustainable agriculture. UCS publications include the twice-yearly magazine *Catalyst*, the quarterly newsletter *Earthwise*, and the reports *Greener SUVs* and *Greenhouse Crisis: The American Response*.

World Resources Institute (WRI)
1709 New York Ave. NW
Washington, DC 20006
(202) 638-6300
fax: (202) 638-0036

The WRI conducts research on global resources and environmental conditions. It holds briefings, seminars, and conferences and provides the print and broadcast media with new perspectives and background materials on environmental issues. The institute publishes reports, papers, and books on energy.

Worldwatch Institute
1776 Massachusetts Ave. NW
Washington, DC 20036-1904
(202) 452-1999
fax: (202) 296-7365

Worldwatch is a research organization that analyzes and calls attention to global problems, including environmental concerns such as energy and oil. It compiles the annual *State of the World* anthology and publishes the bimonthly magazine *World Watch* and the Worldwatch Paper Series, which includes "Clearing the Air: A Global Agenda" and "The Climate of Hope: New Strategies for Stabilizing the World's Atmosphere."

Books

Blundell, Katherine, and Fraser Armstrong, eds. *Energy . . . Beyond Oil.* New York: Oxford University Press, 2007. Focuses on solutions to the energy problem rather than just the problem itself. It describes the major energy-generation technologies currently under development and provides an authoritative summary of the current status of each one.

Corsi, Jerome R., and Craig R. Smith. *Black Gold Stranglehold: The Myth of Scarcity and the Politics of Oil.* Medford, OR: WND, 2005. Argues that it is fraudulent science that has made America believe that oil is a fossil fuel and that it is a finite resource.

Freeman, S. David. *Winning Our Energy Independence.* Layton, UT: Gibbs Smith, 2007. Explains how the sun, wind, biomass, geothermal, and hydrogen resources we have right now can be the fuels that solve energy issues and create a sustainable future for our planet. These alternative energies will heat and cool our homes, run our cars, power our factories, and do all the things that our civilization requires—but only if Americans choose to make it happen.

Goodstein, David. *Out of Gas: The End of the Age of Oil.* New York: W.W. Norton, 2004. Explains the fundamentals of energy, engines, and entropy for a mass audience.

Kambara, Tatsu, and Christopher Howe. *China and the Global Energy Crisis: Development and Prospects for China's Oil and Natural Gas.* Edward Elgar, 2007. Examines China's record of oil and gas development, its refining capacity, and energy prospects. The authors conclude that there are no fundamental reasons for anxiety about China's demands on the world energy economy, but they emphasize that its energy future will depend critically on a continuation of reform and internationalization.

Margonelli, Lisa. *Oil on the Brain: Adventures from the Pump to the Pipeline.* New York: Nan A. Talese/Doubleday, 2007. The story, from beginning to end, of how oil is pumped, traded, refined, distributed, and sold to the public. Covers the conditions, both political and cultural, in a number of oil-producing countries.

Maugeri, Leonardo. *The Age of Oil: The Mythology, History and Future of the World's Most Controversial Resource.* New York: Praeger, 2006. Provides a lively, insightful perspective to the history and condition of the world petroleum industry.

Norman, James R. *The Oil Card: Global Economic Warfare in the 21st Century.* Waterville, OR: TrineDay, 2008. Discusses how oil pricing and availability have a long history of being employed as economic weapons by the United States.

Paul, Bill. *Future Energy: How the New Oil Industry Will Change People, Politics and Portfolios.* New York: Wiley, 2007. Explores investment implications of the new oil industry.

Roberts, Paul. *The End of Oil: On the Edge of a Perilous New World.* New York: Mariner, 2005. Warns that the global supply of oil is being depleted at an alarming rate. Which energy sources will replace oil, who will control them, and how disruptive to the current world order the transition from one system to the next will be are just a few of the big questions that the author attempts to answer.

Rutledge, Ian. *Addicted to Oil: America's Relentless Drive for Energy Security.* New York: I.B. Tauris, 2006. Provides a sweeping account of the forces, policies, and personalities that drive America's unending pursuit of foreign petroleum.

Sandalow, David. *Freedom from Oil: How the Next President Can End the United States' Oil Addiction.* New York: McGraw-Hill, 2007. Takes the reader to the highest levels of government, as cabinet members and White House aides debate how to break America's addiction to oil.

Zubrin, Robert. *Energy Victory: Winning the War on Terror by Breaking Free of Oil.* Amherst, NY: Prometheus, 2007. Argues for a biofuel-based approach to the problem of oil use in the world. Explores benefits for international development that should command the attention of advocates, academics, and policy makers.

Periodicals

Allen, Mike. "Crunching the Numbers on Alternative Fuels," *Popular Mechanics,* May 2006. www.popularmechanics.com/science/earth/2690341.html.

Bailey, Ronald. "Peak Oil Panic: Is the Planet Running Out of Gas?" *Reason,* May 2006.

Bradsher, Keith. "A New, Global Oil Quandary: Costly Fuel Means Costly Calories," *New York Times,* January 19, 2008.

Dalmia, Shikha. "Have You Hugged a Hummer Today?" *Reason,* July 19, 2006. www.reason.org/commentaries/dalmia_20060719.shtml.

Epstein, Alex. "What to Do About Rising Gas Prices," May 24, 2007. www.capmag.com/article.asp?ID=49669.

Feller, Gordon. "China's Energy Demand—Improving Energy Intensity Is Proving a Daunting Task in the World's Most Populous Nation," *EcoWorld,* May 20, 2007. www.ecoworld.com/Home/articles2.cfm?tid=428.

Gordon, John Steele. "Running Out of Oil: The Problem Is as Old as the Industry Itself," *American Heritage,* November/December 2005.

Hauke, Justin P., and Christopher J. Neely. "Asian Nations Driving World Oil Prices," *Regional Economist,* April 2007. http://stlouisfed.org/publications/re/2007/b/pages/oil-prices.html.

Jordan, James, and James Powell. "The False Hope of Biofuels: For Energy and Environmental Reasons, Ethanol Will Never Replace Gasoline," *Washington Post,* July 2, 2006.

Khosla, Vinod. "My Big Biofuels Bet," *Wired,* October 2006.

Lardelli, Michael. "A Revolutionary Report on the Future of Oil," EnergyBulletin.net, July 29, 2007. www.energybulletin.net/32721.html.

Lilly, Scott. "How Much to Feed a Dragon," Center for American Progress, June 13, 2005. www.americanprogress.org/issues/2005/06/b795013.html.

Lydecker, Jim. "Overpopulation and Peak Oil: The Perfect Storm," *Napa Valley Register* (California), January 18, 2008.

Maugeri, Leonardo. "What Lies Below?" *Newsweek* Issues 2007, 2006. www.newsweek.com/id/44204.

Moore, Patrick. "Going Nuclear: A Green Makes the Case," *Washington Post,* April 16, 2006. www.washingtonpost.com/wpdyn/content/article/2006/04/14/AR2006041401209.html.

Osnos, Evan. "The Coming Fight for Oil," *Chicago Tribune,* December 19, 2006.

Pearce, Fred. "Forests Paying the Price for Biofuels," *New Scientist,* November 22, 2005. www.newscientist.com/article.ns?id=mg188 25265.400.

Polk, Eben. "Efficiency Where We Need It," Re:Vision, October 18, 2006. www.revision.org/files/efficiencywhereweneedit.pdf.

Shealy, Malcolm, and James P. Dorian. "Growing Chinese Energy Demand: Is the World in Denial?" Center for Strategic and International Studies, October 2007. www.csis.org/media/csis/pubs/071211-shealy-growingchineseenergy-web.pdf.

Tokkelossi, Christian. "Is Ethanol Worth the Hype?" *New West,* April 27, 2006. www.newwest.net/index.php/main/article/8082.

Tuite, Don. "Can Greens and Nukes Coexist? The Future Probably Involves a Mix of Energy-Generating Technologies," *Electronic Design,* June 29, 2007.

Vidal, John. "The End of Oil Is Closer than You Think," *Guardian,* April 21, 2005. www.guardian.co.uk/life/feature/story/0,13026,1464050,00.html.

Watts, Michael. "Oil Inferno," Counterpunch.org, January 2, 2007. www.counterpunch.org/watts01022007.html.

Wenzel, Elsa. "Nuke Power Not So Green or Clean," CNET.com, June 11, 2007. http://news.com.com/Nuke+power+not+so+clean+or+green/2008-11392_3-6189817.html?tag=st.num.

Whittelsey, Frances Cerra, "Bio-Hope, Bio-Hype," *Sierra,* September/October 2007. www.sierraclub.org/sierra/200709/bio.asp.

Woolsey, R. James, and Anne Korin. "Turning Oil into Salt," *EVWorld,* September 27, 2007. www.evworld.com/article.cfm?storyid=1328.

Web Sites

Alliance to Save Energy (www.ase.org). Promotes energy efficiency worldwide to achieve a healthier economy, a cleaner environment, and greater energy security. Offers K-12 lesson plans, energy-saving tips, and other resources.

The Coming Global Oil Crisis (www.oilcrisis.com). Maintained by editor Ron Swenson, this site contains hundreds of links to articles from reputable sources that discuss the coming global oil crisis.

Fuel Economy (www.fueleconomy.gov). A Web site sponsored by the Department of Energy. It contains extensive information about gas prices, mileage per gallon, hybrid vehicles, and alternative fuel vehicles.

Office of Fossil Energy Homepage (www.fossil.energy.gov). A Department of Energy site dedicated to exploring all aspects of fossil fuel use.

The Oil Drum (www.oildrum.com). This site, maintained by a group of professors and engineers, contains many useful charts and graphics relating to energy and oil issues.

Organization of the Petroleum-Exporting Countries (www.opec.org). OPEC is a cartel of petroleum-exporting countries. As of 2007 its members included Iraq, Indonesia, Iran, Kuwait, Libya, Angola, Algeria, Nigeria, Qatar, Saudi Arabia, the United Arab Emirates, and Venezuela. OPEC's mission is to coordinate and unify the petroleum policies of the member countries and ensure the stabilization of oil markets in order to secure an efficient, economic, and regular supply of petroleum to consumers.

Terror-Free Oil Initiative (www.terrorfreeoil.org). Terror-Free Oil Initiative is dedicated to encouraging Americans to buy fuel that originated from countries that do not export or finance terrorism.

World Without Oil (http://worldwithoutoil.org). An interesting Web site that explores how the world will be affected by declining production of oil by simulating thirty-two weeks of a world without oil. Contains resources for both teachers and students relating to the decline of oil.

Index

A
Air pollution
from diesel vehicles, 86–87
from vehicles, 84–86
Alaska, North Slope, oil spills in,
74
American Petroleum Institute, 27
Arctic National Wildlife Refuge
(ANWR), 7–9
coastal plain, size of, 79
creation of, 71–72
oil drilling will not ruin, 77–82
oil drilling will ruin, 70–76
Argonne National Laboratory, 101
AT-PZEV (Advanced Technology
Partial Zero Emission Vehicles),
93, 96–98
Auerswald, Philip E., 64

B
Bailey, Ronald, 20
Bakhtiar, Ali, 37
Bin Laden, Osama, 8
Bin Talal, Al-Waleed, 61
Biofuels
should not replace oil, 130–136
should replace oil, 124–129
See also Ethanol
Bodman, Samuel, 22
Branson, Richard, 30
Brazil, biofuels production by, 131,
135–136
Broinowski, Richard, 107
Brown, Lester, 131
Bullis, Kevin, 100

Busby, John, 109
Bush, George W./Bush administration, 21–22, 39, 107
on dependence on foreign oil,
61
on estimated revenues from
ANWR development, 82
foreign policy of, 63
hydrogen fuel initiative of, 24

C
California Air Resources Board
(ARB), 87–88
emission ratings by, 93
California Department of
Transportation, 87
Canadian Business (magazine), 38
Carlson, John, 110
Carter administration, 24
China
increase in number of cars in, 42
oil and, 43, 44–46
Clinton administration, 24
Coal
British Empire and, 34
electrical plants and, 120
Council on Foreign Relations, 39

D
Darley, Julian, 11
Deforestation, 131–132, 135–136
Department of Interior, U.S., 9
Developing nations, 40–46
Diesel engines
air pollution from, 86–87
new fuel standards for, 87–88

Picture Credits

AP: 10, 13, 23, 28, 37, 42, 54, 57, 60, 68, 73, 80, 85, 97, 99, 103, 109, 114, 121, 126, 135

Steve Zmina: 15, 21, 31, 35, 44, 51, 62, 66, 79, 89, 94, 102, 115, 128, 133